MANAGING UNCERTAINTY

OTHER ECONOMIST BOOKS

MANAGING UNCERTAINTY

Strategies for surviving and thriving
in turbulent times

Michel Syrett and
Marion Devine

WILEY
John Wiley & Sons, Inc.

Library of Congress Cataloging-in-Publication Data:
ISBN 978-1-118-10319-7 (Hardcover); ISBN 978-1-118-16653-6 (ebk);
ISBN 978-1-118-16651-2 (ebk); ISBN 978-1-118-16652-9 (ebk)

Printed in the United States of America
10 9 8 7 6 5 4 3 2 1

#781681256

To our partners Suzy and Stephen

Contents

Acknowledgements

IN PRODUCING THIS BOOK, we have been helped by a number of individuals and organisations that require acknowledgement.

First and foremost, we would like to acknowledge PA Consulting Group (PA), which undertook in collaboration with the authors a survey of 205 international businesses in spring 2011. The results of this survey provided us with statistical evidence on which to base our conclusions and contact with the majority of the senior executives whom we interviewed for the book.

In particular, we are grateful for the support and encouragement of Mark Thomas, a business strategy expert at PA, instigator of the survey and a published author in his own right on the topic of strategic determination in an age of uncertainty; Jackie Howell, senior global marketing manager; and Melanie Albury, a PA consultant, who oversaw the survey design and analysis.

We would like to acknowledge the support and encouragement of other "thought leaders" on this topic, most notably Donald Sull, a professor at London Business School, and Eric Beinhocker, a senior fellow at the McKinsey Global Institute, who contributed their thoughts and insights to this book.

We would also like to thank the many senior executives who allowed us to interview them for the book. Their names appear throughout the text but the organisations they represent span Ashridge, Balfour Beatty, Capital One Bank, Ceridian, Ford, GlaxoSmithKline, Honda Europe, London Business School, IMI, Marsh, McKinsey, Random House, Royal State of Jersey, Simmons & Simmons, SunGard India, Wipro Infoprocessing and the UK government's Foresight project.

On the editorial side, thanks to Stephen Brough and Penny Williams; and thanks to Sally Harper for her private editing support. Lastly, we would like to thank our partners, Suzy and Stephen, for putting up with long weekends of us being chained to the computer and immersed in mutual deliberation.

Preface

WHEN IN 2009 we first thought of writing a book on managing uncertainty, it was through intellectual curiosity about what our research would reveal.

A wealth of work on the topic had been published in the previous decade, but as much of it was written by academics, it was theoretical and not based on commercial good practice. Much of it was dated and nothing had been written since the global financial crisis that unleashed a new era of uncertainty for organisations to cope with.

Our initial instinct that the 2008 crisis was out of the ordinary proved correct. When it occurred, many senior executives assumed that it was another turn in the boom-and-bust cycle that had characterised macroeconomics in developed economies since the end of the second world war. They reacted accordingly, cutting costs and "hunkering down" for what they supposed would be a painful but short period of austerity.

However, the crisis has ushered in a period of unprecedented uncertainty, with the economic unknowns augmented by political and social unknowns arising from such developments as the Arab spring and the anti-capitalist and anti-austerity protests in a number of developed countries.

Uncertainty is here to stay. Not for nothing did a secretary-general of the United Nations recently comment that the first years of the 21st century may well prove "a decisive moment in the human story", requiring co-operation by politicians and business leaders across all boundaries to respond to the interconnected threats the world currently faces (see Chapter 1).

A book that examined the implications of managing uncertainty in more practical terms seemed overdue when this book was first commissioned. By the time it was written the case was overwhelming.

We wanted to use the research to explore three questions. First, how do business people define uncertainty? – because precise definitions lead to concrete solutions. Second, is managing uncertainty becoming a defined management discipline like change or talent management? Third, what are the implications, not just for strategy determination (the focus of most of the early work on the topic) but for an organisation's overall development and culture?

The feedback gleaned from senior executives interviewed for the book suggests that, in their eyes, there is no precise definition of uncertainty and therefore no precise solution. Some see the task of managing uncertainty as no more than an extension of financial risk management, entailing the need for financial "buffers" brought about by greater liquidity.

Others saw the challenge in broader terms, entailing a more flexible approach to strategy formulation and shorter, more regular reviews of progress and change, using non-financial measures as well as more conventional fiduciary ones. There was no consensus on a distinct and coherent set of skills to help support the task.

The imperative stressed over and over again by the business people we talked to related to an organisation's "strategic readiness" for sudden and unexpected threats and opportunities – through a combination of strategic flexibility, strong navigational leadership, resilience, collaborative partnership, predictive learning and agility. This focus is reflected in the book's structure and conclusions.

Michel Syrett and Marion Devine
June 2012

Introduction: managing in an uncertain world

There are known knowns; there are things we know we know. We also know there are known unknowns; that is to say we know there are some things we do not know. But there are also unknown unknowns – the ones we don't know we don't know.

Donald Rumsfeld, US defence secretary, 2001-06

Historians may well look back on the first years of the 21st century as a decisive moment in the human story. The different societies that make up the human family are today interconnected as never before. They face threats that no nation can hope to master by acting alone – and opportunities that can be much more hopefully exploited if all nations work together.

Kofi Annan, UN secretary-general, 1997-2006

DONALD RUMSFELD GOT IT RIGHT. When he used the above analogy, he was speaking at a press briefing in 2002 about the absence of evidence linking the government of Iraq with the supply of weapons of mass destruction to terrorist groups. His words were criticised at the time as an abuse of language by, among others, the Plain English Campaign. However, Geoffrey Pullum, a linguist, disagreed, saying the comment was "completely straightforward" and "impeccable, syntactically, semantically, logically and rhetorically".

Whatever the rights and wrongs linguistically, the quotation provides a perfect starting point for this book.

We are now living in a world which combines known knowns, known unknowns and unknown unknowns, and the growth of the last category presents business leaders with a new and little-charted management challenge.

At the heart of the traditional approach to strategy lies the assumption that by applying a set of powerful analytical tools, executives can predict the future of any business accurately enough to allow them to choose a clear strategic direction.

But what happens when the environment is so uncertain that no amount of analysis will allow us to predict the future? What makes for a good strategy in highly uncertain business environments? How can organisations prepare themselves for the challenge of anticipating and responding to unanticipated events? What individual and organisational capabilities are required?

The uncertain world order

The need to focus on the challenges of an uncertain world has never been more urgent. Much of the academic and consultancy work undertaken on managing uncertainty was conducted in the 1990s and the first few years of the 21st century and the resulting analysis was largely theoretical. Furthermore, it is now apparent that the research and analysis were carried out during a period when world economies were enjoying what proved to be an Indian summer of growth and stability.

This book will argue, among many things, that the financial crisis of 2008 has proved a watershed. What was originally thought by many organisations to be just another cycle in the boom-and-bust that characterised the post-war era has turned out to be the harbinger of an enduring period of financial instability. This has been accompanied and aggravated by political and social upheaval and environmental crises – all of which have profound implications for international business.

In-depth interviews with 40 senior executives supported by 50 responses to an online survey by the Ashridge Consulting Group in 2010[1] found that business leaders experienced an abrupt and dramatic change in their organisation's environment as a result of the economic downturn. Many of these executives believed this change was likely to persist long after the downturn's immediate effects.

All participants had sufficient experience to be able to recall previous economic downturns. However, they felt that the 2008 crisis was different because of the:

- speed and abruptness of change in their markets;
- depth and magnitude of decline in some markets (such as automotive, property, construction, shipping);
- inconsistency in and unpredictable nature of changes across different sectors;
- breakdown of trust in institutions, particularly financial ones, that had always been considered reliable;
- global nature of the recession such that all regions and most countries had been affected;
- interconnectedness of markets, geographies and institutions;
- lack of availability of credit and finance.

The report's authors commented:

[Business leaders] have been thrown into a world of uncertainty and ambiguity. Any sense of stability in the present or confidence in their ability to predict reliably the future has disappeared ... A wave of anxiety has been unleashed across organisations, markets and society. This reflects a "fear of not knowing".

Ashridge is not alone in this conclusion. Ronald Heifetz, a management thinker, in an article published in *Harvard Business Review* in 2009, concluded:[2]

It would be profoundly reassuring to view the current economic crisis as simply another rough spell that we need to get through. Unfortunately, though, today's mix of urgency, high stakes, and uncertainty will continue as the norm even after the recession ends. Economies cannot erect a firewall against intensifying global competition, energy constraints, climate change, and political instability. The immediate crisis – which we will get through, with the help of policymakers' expert technical adjustments – merely sets the stage for a sustained or even permanent crisis of serious and unfamiliar challenges.

How we ended up in this situation was also described vividly by Mark Thomas, a business strategy expert at PA, and author of *The Zombie Economy* in an interview conducted for this book:

> *I think perhaps we have all been spoiled. The truth is that in some ways, the last 20 years until the crisis were a relatively easy period for managing in. The cost of capital was coming down and down and it was, in theory, ever easier for companies to earn a return above the cost of capital and to generate shareholder value. It was therefore by and large a boom time in the stockmarket. We believed the NICE decade – non-inflationary, continuously expansionary growth – was going to go on forever. In that sense, it was a benign environment for quite a long time.*
>
> *But I think what is happening now is so big that even people who are very experienced are still taken aback by the scale of uncertainty. It is genuinely a difficult time to be managing, even if people have not been spoiled in the last decade. This is genuine uncertainty on a scale none of us have ever seen before. There are very few people out there with useful frames of reference.*

Speed and multiplication

It is worth pinpointing two facets of the turmoil that the world has endured since 2008.

The first is the sheer speed of events and the extent to which they multiply. What began as a bursting of the American housing-market bubble and a rise in foreclosures ballooned rapidly into a global financial and economic crisis. Some of the largest and most venerable banks, investment houses and insurance companies declared bankruptcy or had to be rescued financially. By October 2008 credit flows had frozen, lender confidence had dropped and one after another the economies of countries around the world dipped towards recession.

The second is the knock-on effect the original crisis had on world markets. The crisis exposed fundamental weaknesses in financial systems worldwide. Despite co-ordinated easing of monetary policy by governments, trillions of dollars in intervention by central banks and governments, and large fiscal stimulus packages, the crisis failed to abate.

What began in industrialised countries quickly spread to emerging markets and developing economies. As an American Congressional Report published in October 2009 commented:[3]

> *The global crisis now seems to be played out on two levels. The first is among the industrialised nations of the world where most of the losses from subprime mortgage debt, excessive leveraging of investments, and inadequate capital backing credit default swaps (insurance against defaults and bankruptcy) have occurred.*
>
> *The second level of the crisis is among emerging-market and other economies who may be "innocent bystanders" to the crisis but who also may have less resilient economic systems that can often be whipsawed by actions in global markets.*
>
> *Most industrialised countries (except for Iceland) have been able to finance their own rescue packages by borrowing domestically and in capital markets, but many emerging-market and developing economies have insufficient sources of capital and have turned to help from the International Monetary Fund (IMF), World Bank, or from capital surplus nations, such as Japan, and the European Union.*

Yet the very measures taken by industrialised companies to protect themselves from the effects of the crisis precipitated even bigger problems. Excessive borrowing by governments to finance rescue packages, particularly in the euro zone, led quickly to unmanageable debt. This was aggravated by a lowering of credit ratings by financial institutions and a consequential increase in interest rates.

Convergence and interconnectivity

The steady stream of global upheavals that followed in the wake of the 2008 economic crisis illustrate how events that were previously thought to be unconnected are converging – a fact stressed time and again by executives and others interviewed for this book. (See Appendix for a list of executives' names and job descriptions.)

Eric Beinhocker, a senior fellow at the McKinsey Global Institute, and author of *The Origin of Wealth*, highlighted how the world has always seemed uncertain but that technology has changed perceptions and emotional reactions to uncertainty:

> *If you read history, you have to feel that everybody thought their world was pretty unstable. If you were sitting here in the 1930s, the world would look like a pretty uncertain place and in fact, they would have been right. Each era has its own big issues and effects. What has changed, because of technology, is our ability to understand what is going on around the world and the way this influences our own decisions and actions.*
>
> *Previously in history, your own patch of the world might have felt okay and you would have been blissfully unaware of the great traumas going on in another patch of the world. Sitting here today, London is pretty calm but all sorts of things are happening in the Middle East which are on the news on a 24/7 basis. So our perception and feeling about uncertainty is certainly different.*

World events like the Arab spring of 2011 and the contemporaneous earthquake in Japan that devastated its eastern coast illustrate how interconnected the world has become – and consequently much more uncertain.

As Lewis Booth, executive vice-president and chief financial officer of Ford Motor Company, commented when asked whether we are living in a more uncertain world than in the past:

> *Interdependence has without doubt brought in much more uncertainty. As an example, think of the issues you see arising out of the earthquake in Japan, which is affecting very small suppliers that supply global manufacturers, with the impact rippling around the world affecting any number of large manufacturers. Think also about the consequences of the Arab spring and the impact that this is likely to have not only on the supply and price of oil but on migration and the composition of Middle Eastern markets. The sheer scale of events piling one on top of the other is making business keener to anticipate and respond effectively to the unexpected.*

Dick Nanto, a specialist in industry and trade for the American Congress, explained the consequences in 2009, anticipating both the Arab spring and riots and protests in Europe and the United States:[4]

> *Financial crises impact on political leadership and regimes within countries through two major mechanisms. The first is the discontent from citizens who are losing jobs, seeing businesses go bankrupt, losing wealth both in financial and real assets, and facing declining prices for their products.*
>
> *In democracies, this discontent often results in public opposition to the existing establishment or ruling regime. In some cases it can foment extremist movements, particularly in poorer countries where large numbers of unemployed young people may become susceptible to religious radicalism that demonises Western industrialised society and encourages terrorist activity.*

Looking ahead

Is this period of intense disruption temporary, or will the state of uncertainty of the past half decade persist? A report by Foresight, part of the UK Government Office for Science (see Chapter 2), pinpointed 11 "dimensions of uncertainty", which will determine the political and economic environment in which businesses will operate in the period leading up to 2050.[5]

An important question, for example, is whether increased globalisation will cause countries to veer towards nationalism to protect their power or towards more federal and economic blocs via bilateral and multilateral agreements. Will global economic shocks help create a global model that is laissez-faire or highly regulated? Will future international and civil wars be fought state versus state, state versus non-state, or non-state versus non-state? Who will own and have the right to benefit from scientific and technology-based innovation? Will new communications technologies lead to the emergence of borderless or virtual communities? Will future or continued economic development be contingent upon sustainable development?

The main aim of the report is to show how these dimensions of uncertainty affect each other. For example, the supply of well-educated and trained labour on which business relies is related directly to the interaction between advances in science, technology and innovation (which determine the skills required by industry), the domestic government's education and skills policy (which determines the internal supply of skilled labour) and migration trends and policy (which determine the external supply).

TABLE 1.1 **Dimensions of uncertainty**

1	Balance of power and governance architecture
2	Economic integration, governance and models
3	Security and conflict
4	Science, technology and innovation
5	Education and skills
6	Communities and communities
7	Demographics and migration
8	Health and well-being
9	Climate change
10	Natural resources
11	Values and beliefs

Source: UK Government Office for Science, 2009

If, during a period of rapid technological advance, a government simultaneously cuts back on education and professional training funding and restricts immigration, for economic reasons, there are likely to be shortages of skilled labour in key industries. In a completely different sphere, better-educated individuals are generally more aware of the relationship between lifestyle, diet and health leading to greater consumer demand for products and services supplied by industries that are shaped by or connected to health and well-being.

The report's authors conclude:

Today's problems can be so immediate and all-pervasive that they can act as blinkers which result in a myopic focus on the present, to the exclusion of a more strategic vision of the future. Given that some elements of the future will be profoundly different from those of today, it follows that the shape and purpose of policy and organisations must adapt and change in order to meet the challenges and opportunities of a new strategic environment.

The long-term consequences of the different choices and pathways outlined by the report's authors is explored in greater detail by Foresight's American counterpart, the Rockefeller Foundation, in a 2010 report published in collaboration with the Global Business Network.[6]

The report outlined four possible "world scenarios" in the years leading to 2050, based on the relationship between low or high levels of technological adaptation and weak or strong levels of political and economic alignment. From worst to best, they encompass the following:

■ **Hack attack.** An economically unstable and shock-prone world in which governments weaken, criminals thrive and dangerous innovations emerge. This might encompass:
  - development goals being postponed or abandoned;
  - Islamic terror networks extending to Latin America;
  - international aid agencies forced to scale back;
  - widespread violence against minorities and immigrants;
  - an Indo-Pakistan water war.
■ **Lock step.** A world of tighter government control and more authoritarian leadership, with limited innovation and growing protest from local populations. This might encompass:
  - an African embrace of authoritarian capitalism using the China model;
  - intercontinental trade being hit by strict controls designed to prevent the spread of disease.
■ **Smart scramble.** An economically depressed world in which individuals and communities develop localised, makeshift solutions to a growing set of problems. This might encompass:
  - greater venture-capital spending in sub-Saharan Africa;
  - the development of low-cost water purification devices that halve diarrhoea deaths in Asia;
  - new diagnostic techniques to combat local diseases in developing countries;

- an increase in local protests against government authoritarianism, particularly in China.
■ **Clever together.** A world in which highly co-ordinated and successful strategies emerge from addressing urgent and entrenched worldwide issues. This might encompass:
  - the global economy "turning a corner";
  - the development of cheap solar power;
  - a green revolution designed to combat food shortages;
  - radical American and Chinese emissions targets;
  - the emergence and acceptance of transparent and improved international and domestic governance.

Scenario planning of this kind is now common among government planners and the institutes that support them. Yet given the uncertainties that now beset the world, it is surprising that commercial organisations have not followed suit.

Shell is famous for scenario planning. In looking at its strategy over the medium and long term, its scenario planners are asking similar questions to those posed by planners at Foresight and the Rockefeller Foundation.[7] The company is focusing on a number of specific global issues, including the following:

■ **G20 governance.** Can the G20 take on a meaningful role? Can it evolve into the hub of a networked system of global governance, bringing in other global issues such as climate change?

■ **The China-America relationship.** Can China and America work co-operatively on a range of issues from global economic recovery to energy and climate change? Will the relationship act as a marker or template of the evolving longer-term geopolitical adjustment between established and emerging powers?

■ **New policy paradigms.** How can we build the capitalist model and drive new political energies to move economies on the firm path to recovery?

Shell is not seeking to come up with a crystal ball that will predict when crises affecting the business are likely to occur. Rather, as Jeremy Bentham, vice-president, global business environment, says, it is a matter of turning your thinking into what the critical uncertainties are and planning or allowing for them in your strategic thinking.

New patterns of uncertainty

Arnoud De Meyer is a former professor of management studies at INSEAD, an international business school, and the Judge Institute of Management at Cambridge, and now president of the Singapore Management University. De Meyer anticipated Rumsfeld's analogy when he postulated four types of uncertainty that firms may encounter as separate phenomena or in some form of combination:[8]

■ **Variation** comes from many small influences that cannot be easily anticipated individually; however, the resulting variation from a firm's expected outcome can be identified and managed.

■ **Foreseen uncertainties** are identifiable and understood influences that may or may not occur. This form of uncertainty is often resolved through risk management and scenario planning.

■ **Unforeseen uncertainty** is more difficult to manage as a company is unaware of the event's possibility or has discounted its likelihood. There is no contingency plan in place. This form of uncertainty requires businesses to work more flexibly, employ more novel strategic approaches and work more closely with suppliers and customers on which the firm is most dependent.

■ **Chaos** is where unforeseen events invalidate a firm's basic premise and strategy. The firm's best option is to redefine its objectives and business approach. Organisational learning is at a premium. Managers also have to be resilient yet adaptable, and nimble, creative and clear-headed in assessing the options and deciding what actions to take.

In these circumstances, traditional approaches to strategy, risk and change are no longer appropriate. Among the challenges facing senior executives are the following:

■ **Strategy determination.** The traditional assumption underpinning strategy formulation has been that the future can be predicted through the use of powerful analytical tools and therefore that it is possible to set a clear strategic direction. Now that no amount of analysis will provide a reliable set of indicators about the future, how do you determine strategy when the operating environment is uncertain and potentially volatile?

■ **Strategy execution.** This is still dominated by methods developed in the 1980s with the adoption of total quality management. This presumes that goals are determined at the top and the methods required to achieve these goals are driven downwards through the organisation. The emphasis is to achieve "buy-in" to these methods at middle and junior management levels. However, uncertainty breeds flaws. Internal politics and turf wars are just some of the hidden forces that can distort strategy execution and cause unexpected outcomes.

■ **Risk management.** This is the identification, assessment and prioritisation of risks followed by co-ordinated and economical application of resources to minimise, monitor and control the probability and/or impact of unfortunate events. As such, risk management is a transactional financial discipline. While it is an important tool in managing uncertainty, it is not enough on its own to enable senior executives to set the context of events that are difficult to anticipate or to identify alternative strategies. Nor does risk management enable an organisation to achieve the right level of adaptability and "readiness". It is a reactive rather than proactive process.

■ **Change management.** Conventional change management programmes that often take up to five years to fulfil and are initiated on senior management terms may well be derailed by unpredictable events. Effective communication and consultation with the workforce, early in the process, is crucial to the success of change programmes. Yet senior executives are hampered by the fact that they may no longer have a clear vision of where the organisation will be in five years' time. They are therefore unable to provide the strategic leadership that has been their conventional task during change management programmes.

The essence of this book

The indications are that the current period of disruption and unusual uncertainty will continue, and the aim of this book is to answer the questions that any manager faced with managing uncertainty will want to know the answer to. Chief among them are the following:

- How effective were companies in anticipating and responding to the disruption of the past five years and what changes to strategic planning emerged as a consequence? (Chapter 2)

- Is managing uncertainty the same as risk management? If not, in what way does it differ? (Chapter 2)

- What kind of leadership is required to steer an organisation effectively through periods of uncertainty? (Chapter 3)

- What do "agility" and "resilience" – two organisational capabilities perceived as essential in managing uncertainty – mean in practice? (Chapters 4 and 5)

- What new forms of collaborative working underpin the need to develop closer relationships with customers, employees and strategic partners in order to respond effectively to uncertainty? (Chapter 6)

To help answer these questions, PA Consulting Group (PA), in collaboration with the authors, conducted a survey of 205 senior executives from international companies and public-sector organisations in various countries and regions in spring 2011 (see Figure 1.1). In analysing the data, survey responses were compared with total shareholder return (TSR) for the organisations involved (92 in total). The survey questionnaire, which was also used as the basis for follow-up interviews, is reproduced in the Appendix. The results of the survey (henceforth referred to as the managing uncertainty survey) – are explored in greater detail in Chapters 2–6.

It was clear that the survey respondents were extremely concerned about the scale of the uncertainty affecting their businesses. They recognised that what started as an economic crisis was now a tangle of economic, political and regulatory issues (see Figure 1.2). The combination of these unpredictable risks makes it imperative for businesses to become better at managing uncertainty.

FIG 1.1 **Respondents by country or region, %**

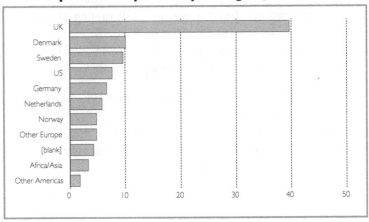

FIG 1.2 **Sources of uncertainty**

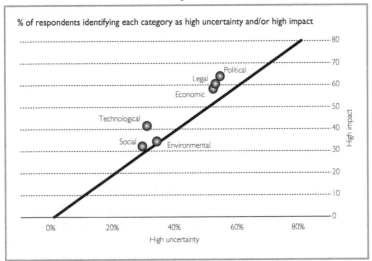

The overriding conclusion of the book is that the ability to manage uncertainty effectively is predicated less on senior executives adopting a set of distinctive management skills – as in the case of risk or change management – and more on inculcating a number of important organisation-wide capabilities that will contribute to a firm's "strategic readiness". Developing this further, there are six capabilities that organisations need to develop: strategic anticipation, navigational leadership, agility, resilience, open collaboration and predictive learning. The following chapters will examine each in turn.

2 Strategic anticipation

The capability to determine and the ability to implement a strategy
that is highly responsive to an unpredictable and potentially volatile
environment

> *The real risk is to be certain about anything.*
>
> Sandy Thomas, Foresight, UK Government Office for Science

> *There is maybe too much rigidity in the American system and
> therefore sometimes it misses the forest for the trees.*
>
> Ravi Kant, vice-chairman, Tata Motors

HOW QUICKLY AND EFFECTIVELY did companies respond to the
financial crisis of 2008? What lessons did they learn about managing
uncertainty? What does this tell us about their ability to anticipate
and respond to uncertainty in the future?

The managing uncertainty survey carried out for this book found
that most companies were late to spot the crisis. They did not believe
the situation was serious until the fall of Lehman Brothers, a financial
services firm, approximately one year after they should have known.
Furthermore, most companies took another six months to respond,
leaving an 18-month gap between observation and action (see Figure
2.1). Speed was a critical factor in how companies measured the
effectiveness of their response. People who thought they made the
right decisions usually made decisions quickly. People who thought
they did not make the right decisions usually did not make decisions
quickly.

The survey also found that the best companies consciously

FIG 2.1 **Awareness of the impact of the financial crises**

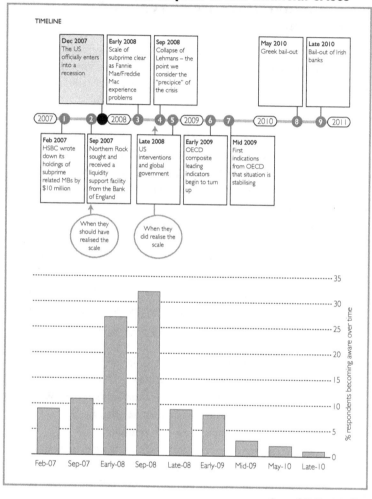

Source: © PA Knowledge 2011

strove to increase their flexibility and responsiveness. Particularly important were flexibility in planning, for example moving from budgets to scenarios; strengthening governance and empowering staff; keeping a keen eye on competitors and an equally keen one on new opportunities, for example acquisitions of struggling businesses.

Global manufacturer's regional subsidiary

We are a large global business but we work in a freestanding way. Our subsidiary is completely autonomous from the global parent company in that we raise our own finance and buy our own systems.

But despite our subsidiary's autonomy, it was in fact always dependent on what happened with the global parent.

When the crisis started to hit, about March 2008, we all felt that we would ride through this as decreasing sales in the region were offset by better sales in other parts of the world.

The crunch came around October. No matter how hard managers tried to turn off the buttons to turn off the flow [of products from the assembly line], and despite the fact that the levers and buttons seemed to be there, they weren't connected to anything. There were no quick responses.

Nobody in our team expected to be in this situation. Usually the decision-making process was consensual, going at a leisurely pace. This situation required urgency but the mechanisms did not respond.

Each country took its decision in isolation from the parent company. So while the regional subsidiary HQ was saying we should stop this, the local organisation was saying, "Well actually I am not too bad here, it must be other people that are having the problem. Therefore I will continue".

So they kept putting in orders and continued as they were. At HQ we started to realise that this was more serious than it appeared and it took the best part of two months to "stop the tanker". The mechanisms just weren't there to stop the process quickly.

Chief executive

People who thought they made the right decisions usually planned flexibly. People who thought they did not make the right decisions

Capital One Bank

We are a large credit-card company with a growing banking service. We are an old-fashioned retail bank. We have no investment banking presence and no involvement in market-backed securities or other opaque securities. As a result, we were well-placed to weather the storm.

We were able to stick to our core business and stay close to our clients. Equally, we were able to raise capital before the crisis came. In 2005, we reduced our reliance on wholesale funding when the CEO said, with remarkable foresight, "I don't want to rely on wholesale funding for my credit-card portfolio".

He made acquisitions so we would have access to a core group of deposits. As a result, when the crisis did hit, we didn't need to raise additional capital from shareholders. We are now one of the consolidators. We bought a bank (Chevy Chase Bank) in Maryland and we are now in the process of completing the acquisition of ING Direct, making Capital One the largest bank in the United States.

The crisis presented us with opportunities and threats. It was an opportunity for the bank to grow and make acquisitions, but clearly market turmoil and the conditions for our clients have not been helpful. The interest-rate environment has also meant that it has been difficult to make money and find decent loan opportunities.

Yes, crisis does present an opportunity when you are able to take advantage of market situations. There have been clear winners from the crisis such as JPMorgan and Capital One Bank, which have been able to make acquisitions in the fallout.

Iain Worsley

usually did not plan flexibly. Moreover, people who thought they made the right decisions were generally those who saw the crisis as an opportunity rather than a threat. However, only a third of companies

---

RBS

At the executive level, all the bank's senior managers have taken part in a programme of strategic value creation. This was in response to a serious concern that in an effort to respond to the crisis of recent years, we would implement short-term temporary cuts and changes that would cause long-term damage.

We had invested a lot of time in recruiting and developing senior executives. We introduced the concept of red and blue line thinking, pioneered by Kevin Kaiser, a professor at INSEAD, which discouraged people from advocating short-term temporary cuts in response to the immediate crisis without thinking about what the long-term impact might be in terms of value creation. (See Chapter 4 for a more detailed summary of red and blue line thinking.)

It was really about getting our executives to take a step back and think about the bigger picture – and we called it "thoughtful execution".

Donna Hamilton

---

saw crisis in this way, with two-thirds stating that they would put more effort into following up unexpected opportunities thrown up by future crises. It was clear that the best-performing companies were also the ones that viewed the crisis as an opportunity.

Lastly, the survey found that the best companies had a moderate approach to cost reduction and shrinkage. Over 80% of companies undertook some form of cost reduction. But the most successful were measured and focused. They did not cut excessively. They tried to preserve staff. They avoided fire sales of businesses at the trough.

Three issues are worth exploring in more detail:

- flexibility;
- integration;
- decision-making.

Flexible planning

In the managing uncertainty survey, the need for plans that are adaptable and can be adapted quickly was one of the most important lessons learned by respondents. Just over half the organisations surveyed employ flexible planning and another quarter intend to do so in future.

As Mark Thomas of PA Consulting Group comments:

Most management tools are geared for a world which faces predictable risk and not too much uncertainty. It is quite a difficult challenge when it comes to managing genuine uncertainty and I think people do flip into a crisis mode in many cases.

The problem is that people manage a lot by experience ... For example, for 20 years you have managed through business cycles that have been traditional inventory cycles of booms and bust. You have a set of tools, for example budgets and forecasts and three-year plans, all of which have more or less served you well. When something like the current turbulence happens, it is difficult to throw those tools away and ask, "what are the tools I need for managing uncertainty?" The temptation is to try and use those same tools in a different way.

By way of illustration, I have talked to managers about their use of scenario planning. They have asked "does that mean I should be putting in plus or minus 10% into our budgets?" as if it is a risk management exercise. I responded that it is not about putting a number into your budgets, it is about thinking through major qualitative changes in the world. For example, the potential collapse or fragmentation of the euro zone is not captured by a single number, 10% up or down.

They really struggle with this and say "this is not helpful to me because I need a number to put into my planning process". I think there are still a lot of people who are desperately trying to use the same tools for a purpose for which they are no longer fit.

It is difficult to learn lessons but harder still to unlearn things. If you have a set of tools you have mastered over a period of years, it is psychologically difficult to say these are just inappropriate now and I need to be looking at these issues in new ways. It

is psychologically very difficult to do this, even when it is not
particularly hard to learn to use more appropriate tools for
managing uncertainty.

Eric Beinhocker of the McKinsey Global Institute and author of
The Origin of Wealth concurs:

If you look at the strategic plans of most companies, they have
some set of scenarios and financial projections, some discounting
back according to cost and capital, comparing scenario A and
scenario B. This is the standard tool that most consulting firms
champion. However, it eliminates the possibility of low probability
but big impact events. We know that the world is increasingly full
of these events – the financial crash of 2008 and what is going on
in the Middle East right now being two very good examples. These
methods don't take into account the notion that many events in the
world have consequences that are irreversible – that time doesn't run
backwards.

Beinhocker's colleague at McKinsey, Hugh Courtney, was arguing
as far back as the late 1990s that the traditional approach to strategic
planning leads executives to view uncertainty in a "binary" way. They
assume that the world is either certain, and therefore open to precise
predictions about the future, or uncertain, and therefore completely
unpredictable:[1]

Underestimating uncertainty can lead to strategies that neither
defend against the threats nor take advantage of the opportunities
that higher levels of uncertainty may provide ... At the other extreme,
assuming that the world is entirely uncertain can lead managers to
abandon the analytical rigour of their traditional planning processes
altogether and base their strategic decisions primarily on gut
instinct.

In an article published in the *Harvard Business Review* in 1997,[2]
Courtney and his fellow consultants Jane Kirkland and Patrick
Viguerie outlined how strategic planning can be tailored to different
types of uncertainty. They identified four types of uncertainty:

- **A clear enough future.** A single forecast precise enough for determining strategy. In these circumstances, the traditional strategic approach of laying out a vision of the future precise enough to be captured in a discounted cash-flow analysis will work effectively.

- **Alternate futures.** A few discrete outcomes that define the future. In these circumstances, decision analysis, option valuation and game theory can be used to inform the right decisions.

- **A range of futures.** A range of possible outcomes but no natural scenarios. In these circumstances, technology forecasting and scenario planning can be used to inform the right decisions.

- **True ambiguity.** No basis to forecast the future. In these circumstances, strategists need to fall back on analogies and pattern recognition.

Using these techniques, Courtney, Kirkland and Viguerie argue that organisations can adopt one of three strategic postures.

Lead

In stable commercial environments, companies seek to shape the future, playing a leadership role in shaking up how their industries operate by setting standards, creating demand or by seeking to control the direction of the market in industries with a higher level of uncertainty.

Adapt

Organisations adapt to the future, winning through speed, agility and flexibility in recognising and capturing opportunities in existing markets and, in industries with higher levels of uncertainty, recognising and responding effectively to unexpected market developments.

Wait

Organisations reserve the right to play, investing sufficiently to "stay in the game" but avoiding premature commitments. This involves making incremental investments now that put an organisation in a privileged position through either superior information and cost structures or relationships between customers and suppliers. This allows an organisation to wait until the environment becomes less uncertain before formulating a strategy.

Within this framework companies can use the following techniques and responses.

Option evaluation

This is a structured and costed approach for evaluating strategic options. It provides managers with a consistent assessment of those open to them, based on criteria that reflect the requirements of the business.

Each option is evaluated against a limited number of criteria that will help managers distinguish between their relative benefits and risks. These might include the dangers involved in pursuing the new direction, the financial investment required, the attitude of investors or sponsors, the length of time required to achieve a payback and the resources required in terms of equipment, technology and human talent.

Specific issues the executive team might like to consider include the following:

- **Difficulties.** These might include the capacity, capability and expertise required and whether new collaborative partnerships will need to be forged to pursue this; the degree of organisational difficulty (high, medium or low) and whether wholly new business units or subsidiaries will be required; obtaining buy-in and support internally, and the implications for talent management, training and organisational development. There may also be legal or purchasing issues such as competition rules or the need to find new suppliers. And any difficulties posed by current or potential markets need to be considered.

- **Risks.** When undertaking an options evaluation it is also necessary to consider risk in terms of both potential impact and probability. List the risks inherent in each option and indicate probability and impact (high, medium or low). Those risks with

GlaxoSmithKline

Flexible planning is more of a priority for us now. It is much more possible nowadays for an entrant to come in from another market and completely change the model you have relied on. That ambiguity is driving us towards using strategic planning for a variety of options – so I know I am going to do something now that is going to last for a year and I know in a year's time that I have options A, B or C. I am not going to make this choice explicit to the company today, although I know in a year's time that I am going to have to make that decision.

This has the effect of shortening the strategic cycle, with more regular reviews of the options we are considering.

Adrian Rawcliffe

medium to high impact and probability need addressing and can be used to further distinguish between options.

- **Weighting.** To clarify the decision-making process it is helpful to weight the different factors in order to get the difficulties, risks and aims in proportion.

- **Formalise the decision-making process.** Group dynamics often force a suboptimal decision or prevent any decision from being made. In groups, decisions can create conflict, acrimony and power plays. There is therefore great value in an agreed decision-making process that forces the expression of assumptions and value judgments and addresses all the critical variables in the right order. This can reveal variables that may not otherwise be considered and foster rapid agreement with minimal conflict. It can also ensure the right decision is made and prepare the way for successful implementation.

The Signtific project

The Signtific project, another version of game theory in action, is designed to engage scientists around the world in anticipating the most important innovations and disruptions in science and technology – and understanding their implications for the future.

Designed and run by the Institute for the Future (IFTF), a California-based research centre, the project has run several online "massively multiplayer forecasting games". The IFTF believes this approach to forecasting will "reshape the practice of science over the next few decades" through the use of:

- an open-source approach to identify and aggregate signals of potential scientific innovations and disruptions;
- social media to engage both professional scientists and science enthusiasts;
- interactive games that enable scientists to share their knowledge and collaborate on specific topics of exploration.

The Signtific project operates in three ways. First, a website enables scientists and other interested individuals to post their forecasts or what they perceive as signals about important developments in science and technology. Second, insights from the website are used as the basis for workshops, which focus on a particular geography or "ethnographic niche". Third, the Signtific Laboratory, an open-source platform, uses mass gaming to engage scientists and the public in "thought experiments" about leading-edge developments.

Game theory

Game theory is another commonly used method to evaluate options when organisations are facing a variety of different possible futures. It enables managers to put themselves in the position of their likely competitors, collaborators and stakeholders.

Game theory dates back to 1944 when John Von Neumann, a

A "massively multiplayer forecasting game" focuses on a specific theme, for example what might happen if micro-satellites (used by scientists to run space experiments) were cheap and commercially available to all. An introductory video sets the context. Gamers then play with a set of cards. Each card has a one-sentence "micro-forecast", either positive or negative. Players provide ideas and add to ideas, and also receive points when an idea is developed by other gamers or designated as a "lab favourite".

Peer recognition is the main form of incentive. Depending on their contribution (such as their micro-forecast earning the most points, or being built on most), players earn honorary achievement rewards. This could be the Stephen Hawking award for "the micro-forecast for the clearest sense of the very big picture" or the Ventner award for making the "biggest paradigm shift".

The IFTF has run several forecasting games in co-operation with academic and business organisations. The "free space" programme, for example, was run in Germany, the United States (California) and New Zealand. Over 600 individuals participated and generated 3,466 cards which helped subject experts collate the cards and synthesize the ideas to identify the most significant forecasts.

mathematician, and Oskar Morgenstern, an economist, published their seminal book *Theory of Games and Economic Behaviour*, which provided a systematic way to understand the behaviour of players in situations where their fortunes are interdependent.

In their book *Co-opetition*, business game theorists Adam Brandenburger and Barry Nalebuff comment:[3]

The primary insight of game theory is the importance of focusing on others – of putting yourself in the shoes of other players and trying to play out all the reactions to their actions as far ahead as possible. By adopting this perspective, a company may, for example, discover that its chances for success are greater if it creates a win-win, rather than a win-lose, situation with other players. In other words, companies should consider both co-operative and competitive ways to change the game.

Brandenburger and Nalebuff argue that in game theory, to every action there is a reaction. To analyse how other players will react to your move, you need to play out all the potential reactions (including yours) to their actions as far ahead as possible. You have to look forward far into the game and then reason backwards to figure out which of today's actions will lead you to where you want to end up.

In their co-opetition version of game theory, the players are the organisation itself, customers and suppliers, and two other categories, "substitutors" and "complementors":

- **Substitutors** are alternative players from whom customers may purchase their resources. Brandenburger and Nalebuff argue that Coca-Cola and PepsiCo are substitutors with respect to consumers because they sell rival beverages. A little less obvious is how Coca-Cola and Tyson Foods are substitutors with respect to suppliers – because both use carbon dioxide. Tyson uses it to freeze chickens and Coca-Cola uses it for carbonation.

- **Complementors** are players from whom customers buy complementary products or to whom suppliers sell complementary resources. Hardware and software companies work as complementors because faster hardware increases users' willingness to pay for more powerful software. Rival airlines are substitutors in respect to passengers but they are complementors when they decide to update their fleets because manufacturers can recoup the cost of a new aircraft design only when they have enough airline customers.

In co-opetition, to change the game, you have to change one or more of these elements: who plays, who adds value to the game, custom and practice (there are no universal set of rules), tactics or scope – the boundaries currently respected by the players.

Futures forecasting

Futures forecasts that are in the public domain can be useful for any organisation in its own scenario planning. The UK government's forecasting unit, Foresight, was set up in 1994 with the particular aim of improving the performance of UK science and engineering but also to be of use to society as a whole.

Foresight is also responsible for the Horizon Scanning Centre, created in 2005, to feed this kind of futures work into all government departments. So far it has carried out 30 short projects with 20 different departments to introduce horizon scanning – the process of gathering information about future trends and assessing their significance – in a wide range of policy areas.

Foresight's director, Sandy Thomas, stresses that the most important aspect of Foresight's research is that it crosses traditional boundaries and therefore opens up new thinking:

> We place a great emphasis on multidisciplinary work, involving scientists and researchers from very different fields. There are not many polymaths who can think beyond their own discipline and you are generally dismissed as a dilettante if you do cross your own boundaries. Our job is therefore to stack a lot of areas together and encourage a genuine dialogue between experts who would not normally come into contact with each other. It is really hard to do but the resulting synthesis of thought is unique.

Scenario planning

A good way for organisations to achieve what Thomas is advocating is through the use of scenario planning. This involves coming up with a range of possible future scenarios for the organisation, examining the effects they may have, and then identifying and evaluating possible responses the organisation can make.

Shell is the company most famous for its use of scenario planning in the early 1970s when it anticipated a dramatic increase in the price of oil, as happened in the wake of the Yom Kippur war in 1973. The company's latest set of scenarios, *Signals and Signposts*, published in 2011, covers energy scenarios up to 2050.[4] Among the scenarios the report includes are greater economic volatility; a shift in geopolitical and economic power from West to East; a shift in the make-up of global groupings such as the G7, G10 and G20 and the effect that may have on global governance; and a shift in the relationship between China and the United States. Such scenarios have enabled Shell to engage in contingency planning for all these eventualities.

Jeremy Bentham, vice-president, global business environment, at Shell, stresses that the continual use of scenario planning by senior executives – which has resulted in the technique becoming embedded in the company's culture – has significantly altered the decision-making mindset and made decision-makers better at anticipating and responding to unexpected opportunities or crises.

> *There are four reasons for undertaking this kind of work. One is to make wiser, more robust decisions. The second is that through exploring scenarios, you gain an idea of new opportunities and new threats that you would not have seen otherwise. Third, it helps senior executives to have an awareness of the types of signals and signposts that they may look at in their own circumstances. Scenario planning provides a language for interpreting and hence helps us become more responsive and flexible.*
>
> *Fourth, specifically in terms of human resource development, we aim to build up over time a leadership which is "strategically humble" in the sense of understanding that there are many things that are influencing them and that in order to address these, leaders need to look through the eyes of others. This helps them to see how those patterns of behaviour and choice may be different from what they would assume and recognise that there is a breadth of outcome over which they are not in control.*

Shell's ability to time its new investments and business initiatives more favourably is a direct by-product of the company's use of scenario planning.

> *Timing is always the most uncertain element of these things. You look at pressures but also what you can understand about the*

Defence technology manufacturer

A big hurdle for the company has been our MBO (management by objectives) strategic framework, which spans one year only. This is too short for us to engage in discussions about the future. The focus is on achieving annual targets, not envisaging the future.

We used scenario planning in a recent programme on innovation for 30 senior managers from across our international business. The aim was to help these managers think more broadly about innovation – to see it as more than technical or product development.

The programme introduced new concepts and also a new language of innovation. Scenario planning proved a very useful tool for opening up the minds of our senior managers and engaging them more effectively in planning the future of the business.

Learning and development manager

natural time frames of things. If you look at what needs to happen for new energy technologies once they are proven, in terms of commercial scale and a potential impact at global level, you find that you are talking in terms of at least three decades for something to have a 1% or 2% impact.

When you then look at how quickly that can happen, you are actually looking at questions like how fast can new factories be built and how much time will it take for people to see the performance of a new scale-up before they will invest in the next level of technology.

We believe, for example, that in time vehicle electrification is going to be very significant in the world. Commentators will respond immediately "oh, doesn't this destroy your business?" but we are as much a gas company as an oil company and gas is just one route to providing energy, so we may well end up producing more electricity.

Pattern recognition

Pattern recognition enables managers to pick "meaning" from the huge quantity of information they receive about the environment in which they operate on social, economic and political trends, market developments, competitor activity, suppliers and other stakeholders, and so on.

Phiroz Bhagat, author of *Pattern Recognition in Industry*, explains:

Today we are being deluged by an enormous amount of data. At the same time technical and business fronts are advancing exponentially. Ideally, the endless flow of data should be one of our major assets. However, this potential asset often tends to overwhelm rather than enrich. Competitive advantage depends on the ability to extract and utilise nuggets of valuable knowledge and insight from this data deluge.

Pattern recognition technology helps capture knowledge directly from the plethora of available data, leading to enhanced decision-making and strategy development. This approach has wide applicability in areas ranging from manufacturing processes, product performance and scientific research to financial and business strategy development.

Examples of pattern recognition methodology that are used to assist strategy development for complex situations or in uncertain conditions are as follows:

- **Self-organising systems**, which characterise and cluster data to quantify similarities and differences between previously encountered situations and novel or uncertain ones.
- **Data-driven adaptive learning modelling**, thereby capturing knowledge by building models directly from all available data.
- **Genetic algorithms**, which explore the operating space and so enable the discovery of optimal operating strategies that enhance performance and profitability.

Some ways in which pattern recognition is used by organisations include the following:

- **Customer relationship management.** Pattern recognition can be used in analysing which products or services are most in demand and predicting customers' future buying habits. It can also be used in identifying and mitigating issues that might lose customers or reduce the organisation's ability to gain new ones.

- **Cross-selling.** For an organisation that offers multiple products, an analysis of customers' spending, their use of the product or service and other behaviour through pattern recognition can lead to efficient and timely cross-selling of products.

- **Customer retention.** Traditionally, organisations respond to customer dissatisfaction reactively, after a customer has started the process of terminating their relationship with the business. At this stage, the chance of reversing the customer's decision is negligible. Proper application of pattern recognition in terms of the customer's past service usage, service performance, spending and other behaviour patterns can determine the likelihood of that customer wanting to terminate the relationship sometime in the future, allowing the organisation to intervene when it will make a difference.

- **Fraud detection.** As recent events in the banking industry have shown, fraud is a big problem for many organisations and can be of various types: inaccurate credit applications, fraudulent transactions (both offline and online), identity theft and false insurance claims are some examples. Pattern recognition can be used as part of a predictive model designed to determine a business's exposure to fraud, for example to allow auditors to gauge a company's relative risk and to increase audit procedures to pinpoint the problem.

- **Risk management.** Pattern recognition can be used to predict the likely results of pursuing a future scenario as part of a long-term strategy (see above).

See Chapter 7 for a more detailed exploration of pattern recognition, data mining and analytics.

The Singapore government's RAHS System

Peter Ho, head of Singapore's civil service and permanent secretary at the Ministry of Foreign Affairs, described moving from using scenario planning to adopting tools that placed the organisation in a better state of "strategic anticipation".

My view was that we had entered a period of rapid change and greater complexity. Bear in mind that this was after 9/11 and that in this part of the world, we were still experiencing the political and economic aftershocks of the 1997 Asian financial crisis.

Pattern recognition provided me with the most useful insight: that we were no longer operating in just simple or complicated spaces, where events were more predictable and cause and effects were clearer. Instead we were operating in complex and chaotic domains, where the first to discern patterns out of chaos would have the competitive advantage.

The Civil Service's Risk Assessment and Horizon Scanning (RAHS) system revolves around several key processes: building models, collecting data and organising information; detecting emerging trends and discovering anomalous patterns; and collaborating with other analysts across government in a classified network.

The system has incorporated different approaches to horizon scanning. The resultant diversity will reduce the possibility of getting blindsided by overly relying on one particular approach or one way of thinking about the future.

Integrating strategy determination and execution

One of the most important points to emerge from the managing uncertainty survey was that how strategy is determined can no longer be separated from how it is implemented because of the speed needed to exploit opportunities in an uncertain environment.

In the experience of Damien McKinney of McKinney Rogers, a consulting firm, the speed with which strategy is implemented is hampered in many organisations for a number of important reasons:

- **The target audience for the strategy is not static.** A large organisation can turn around a working population the size of a small town during a five-year change programme.
- **The goalposts change.** Politics (big and small), egos, personalities, misunderstood intentions, turf wars, silo thinking and changing organisational circumstances all combine to change priorities and push the strategy down blind alleys.
- **Poor operational accountability is rife.** Either the goals do not reflect the mission or people are not held accountable to them.
- **Necessary information is imperfect.** It isn't there, or it is not clear, or it is processed and interpreted differently by different people.

Recent research paints a more detailed picture of what goes wrong. A 2003 survey by the Economist Intelligence Unit, in collaboration with Marakon Associates, an international strategy-consulting firm, suggests that companies on average deliver only 63% of the financial performance their strategies promise.[5]

Even worse, the survey found, the causes of this strategy-to-performance gap are all but invisible to senior management. As Michael Marakon, the firm's founder, comments:

> Leaders pull the wrong levers in their attempts to turn around performance – pressing for better execution when they actually need a better strategy, or opting to change direction when they really should focus the organisation on execution. The result is wasted energy, lost time and continued underperformance.

Rainer Feurer, senior vice-president, corporate strategy and planning, at BMW Group, and Kazem Chaharbaghi, a professor at Royal Docks Business School, University of East London, have identified five principles that need to be followed if strategy determination and execution are to be effectively integrated:[6]

- Strategy must be treated as part of individual responsibilities throughout the organisation rather than a central function.

■ In highly dynamic and uncertain environments, competitiveness must be regarded as a multidimensional construct comprising customer values, shareholder values and the organisation's ability to act and react.

■ The internal environment must provide a high degree of stability, while at the same time offering flexibility to respond quickly to change.

■ The quality of a formulated strategy depends on the quality of knowledge used. This in turn hinges on how effectively the process of gaining knowledge is managed. Strategy formulation must therefore be regarded as a constant learning process and the quality of strategy depends on the quality of the organisation's cognitive and behavioural learning mechanisms.

■ The speed at which strategic change can be achieved depends on the speed of strategy formulation together with the way strategy is determined in the organisation through collective collaboration and consultation.

Strategy and innovation: a tale of two companies

These principles are most effective in developing strategies where growth in market share is linked to innovation in either product development or management methods – both important capabilities in responding quickly to unexpected opportunities or threats.

The examples of Tata Group and Procter & Gamble show how this has been put into practice. The strategies adopted by the two companies are predicated on clearly identified priorities, which are supported by the deployment of the right resources and foster a risk-free culture that encourages freedom of action as long as it supports strategic goals.

Tata Group

Tata is a rapidly growing group based in India with significant international operations. Ratan Tata's mission in his final years as chairman was to foster innovation. He started an annual competition with a prize for the best failed idea ("failure is a 'gold mine' for a great company", he says). He also created five clusters (plastics and composites, nanotechnology, engineering, IT and water) that bring together people from different operations.

The group is pursuing innovation on two levels. At the high end, Tata Chemicals is conducting research in nanotechnology and food science, and Tata Consultancy Services (TCS) holds regular innovation conferences in Silicon Valley. But what has attracted more attention is the group's commitment to "frugal innovation": new products to appeal to poor people and the rising middle class.

Tata's best-known frugal product, the Tata Nano, a Rs150,000 ($2,750) rupee car, has run into problems. Some cars have suffered from what Ravi Kant, vice-chairman of Tata Motors, calls "thermal incidents" (what his customers call "catching fire"). Distribution has been poor, although more are appearing on the road. The chief executive of Tata Motors admitted in spring 2011 in Geneva that the Nano business model is having to be reinvented.

Even if the Nano proves disappointing, the idea of frugal innovation looks promising. Tata Motors is making small trucks that are replacing three-wheelers. Tata Chemicals has co-produced a cheap water filter, the Swach, using ingredients such as rice husks. Tata Steel has made a prototype of a $500 house that can be bought in a shop. Taj Hotels is building cheap ($20 a night) hotels for India's army of commercial travellers.

The group is learning to combine the strengths of its various parts. Three companies collaborated on the Swach. After the Asian tsunami in December 2004, TCS and Tata Teleservices joined forces to develop a weather-alert system for fishermen. The group is also engaging in both high-end and low-end innovation. A supercomputer in Pune was built in six weeks for around £30m ($48m), while TCS has created a cheap software package that can teach adults to read in 40 hours.

Interviewed in 2008, Kant contrasted the approach to strategy formulation and execution adopted by his own company with those of US counterparts:[7]

> *There is maybe too much rigidity in the American system and therefore sometimes it misses the forest for the trees. This is not helpful to American companies in the current global situation in which there is so much uncertainty and unpredictability in the environment, in the market and among consumers.*

*If you don't have flexibility in the system, if you don't
keep forcing a review of what is happening, it is very hard for
organisations to move forward on a sustainable basis. Going
forward, all organisations will be required to take some risks and to
exhibit a bit of entrepreneurship that needs to be displayed not just
at the top of the organisation but at lower levels too.
Today's business climate requires a collective and collaborative
system. It's more than any one person can make happen, especially
in a business system that tends to be too rigid.*

Procter & Gamble

Despite difficult market conditions across its global business, Procter &
Gamble (P&G) announced in October 2009 a new long-term "purpose
inspired growth strategy", in the words of its chief executive, Bob
McDonald. The company aims to grow its organic sales 1–2% faster
than market growth in the product categories and countries in which
it competes. To do this, it needs to improve and accelerate internal
innovation. The whole company, not just the extensive research and
development function (P&G invests $2 billion a year in R&D), must
be involved in generating new growth opportunities and improving
existing products through innovation.

P&G's strategy is tightly linked to its stated purpose of "touching
and improving the lives of our customers". McDonald believes
that a "purpose inspired growth strategy" motivates employees to
become more innovative. Launching the strategy in October 2009,
he commented:

*People will innovate for financial gain or for competitive advantage,
but this can be self-limiting. There needs to be an emotional
component as well – a source of inspiration that motivates people.*

P&G has linked its plan for growth with its corporate purpose by
telling its employees where growth needs to come from in its product
categories and markets. It has identified four types of innovation to
increase growth:

■ **Sustaining innovation** to create incremental improvements to
   existing products.

■ **Commercial innovation** to use creative marketing, promotional and packaging approaches to increase sales of existing products.

■ **Transformational-sustaining innovation** to "reframe" products, as Bruce Brown, P&G's chief technology officer, explains: "They typically bring order-of-magnitude improvements and fundamental changes to a business. This type of innovation often leads to breakthroughs in market share, or profit levels." As an example, Brown cites the highly successful launch of Olay Pro-X, a skin-cream product, which generated first-year sales of $50m in American stores alone.

■ **Disruptive innovation**, which enables the company to create a new business with a new offering that is disruptive in the sense that it is simpler, more convenient, easier to access or more affordable compared with existing products or services.

All parts of P&G are expected to search for growth opportunities through these different types of innovation. Senior executives have worked hard to convince managers and employees that the growth strategy is not separate from running the core business, even when trading conditions are tough. Brown explains:[8]

Leaders sometimes see efforts to boost new growth as completely distinct from efforts to bolster the core ... Our experience indicates the opposite. First, new growth efforts depend on a healthy core business. A healthy core produces a cash flow that can be reinvested in new growth. Second, a core business is rich in capabilities that can support new growth efforts. Third, some of the tools for managing core efforts – particularly those that track a project's progress – are also useful for managing new growth efforts.

P&G has a number of training modules to help foster internal innovation. There are modules for senior managers that help them understand the mindsets and behaviours that foster innovation, particularly disruptive innovation. Step-by-step business guides with tools and templates are available to help teams run innovation projects. There are experts across the organisation to support teams working on some form of growth opportunity.

To maintain momentum and avoid a proliferation of small projects, managers can use "portfolio optimisation tools" to help them kill the least promising projects and nurture those with the most potential. These tools allow managers to create projections for ideas and to estimate their financial potential compared with the required human and capital investment. The evaluation method used depends on the type of project, and includes net present value calculations, a risk-adjusted real-option approach, or, if appropriate, qualitative criteria. Brown explains the value of a portfolio approach:

It sets up the expectation that different projects will be managed, resourced and measured in different ways. Also, seeing the portfolio as a whole highlights the critical importance of these activities, which protect and extend core businesses. A portfolio approach also helps reinforce the message that any project, particularly a disruptive one, may carry substantial risk and might not deliver commercial results – and that's fine, as long as the portfolio accounts for the risk.

The linking of purpose, growth and innovation means P&G has had to change its approach to how it develops and reviews strategy. Innovation was always seen as separate from strategy, but the company has now integrated these two streams of activity. Senior managers now work together to integrate the company, business and innovation strategies into a single overarching strategy.

P&G remains firmly committed to its strategy. In 2010, one year after the launch of the new strategy, organic sales grew by 3% and core earnings per share by 6%.

McDonald told shareholders that the company's "purpose inspired growth strategy has helped accelerate business performance". In April 2012, P&G announced sales growth of 2% to $20.2 billion for the January–March quarter; organic sales increased 3%. McDonald says:

We delivered broad-based organic sales growth, with all our business segments growing, in a difficult macroeconomic and competitive environment. We are making good progress against our productivity and cost-savings programme and improving core operating profit growth as we continue to execute our innovation and portfolio expansion plans.

3   Navigational leadership

The capability to instil a collective sense of where the organisation is and the confidence and optimism to move forward into an uncertain future

Employees and management need to believe that there is strong leadership so that their products and services will survive at a time when the company may be struggling. It is a matter of instilling strong faith in the future.

Daniel Galvao, Marsh

I feel my job as a leader has always been to set the goal and then get out of the way.

Praful Pillay, SunGard India

THE MANAGING UNCERTAINTY SURVEY carried out for this book revealed some important findings about leadership and decision-making. In particular:

- people who thought they, or the management team, had made the right decisions instilled stronger leadership and governance, whereas people who thought they didn't make the right decisions tended not to;
- people who thought they made the right decisions empowered, enabled and mobilised staff, whereas people who thought they didn't make the right decisions tended not to;
- people who thought they made the right decisions focused on recruiting and developing talent.

Moreover, a significant proportion of those who did not place great emphasis on these things at the moment stated that they would do so in the future (see Table 3.1).

TABLE 3.1 **Leadership priorities (%)**

	Now	In the future
Building capability and recruiting/developing talent	46	77
Empowering, enabling and mobilising staff	54	73

Source: © PA Knowledge 2011

Strong leadership can make the difference between success and failure at any time, but in uncertain times, as the survey confirms, it is seen as an essential capability. If leadership is not exerted from the top, fear about the future and an accompanying apathy will undermine the organisation's ability to steer its way through the fog.

But what leadership qualities are most important? Traditionally, employees and management have looked to business leaders to provide a strong vision of the future. This applies not only in calm times but, exceptionally, during periods of crisis. But what if uncertainty results in an unclear vision of the future?

Mark Thomas of PA Consulting Group highlighted the dilemma:

There is a huge dilemma for leaders because they have two key jobs: one is management and one is leadership. I think Peter Drucker said that the output of management is decisions, so a CEO is trying to take the right decisions.

Therefore ideally you want to be rational. In this environment, being rational means fully accepting the amount of uncertainty that is out there, not hiding away from it or pretending you know more than you do. Being rational means you face that uncertainty fair and square.

However, leadership demands that you engage people and give them a sense of direction, motivate them, encourage them and paint a picture of an attractive future. This is almost impossible to reconcile fully with that whole-hearted acceptance of uncertainty. I think that is a very profound challenge for top leadership. The same applies at lower levels of the organisation but clearly the bigger the issue, the higher up the organisation people look for the answer and ultimately they look to CEOs to lead the company.

Adrian Rawcliffe, senior vice-president, worldwide business development for R&D, at GlaxoSmithKline, was just one of the many senior executives interviewed for the book to refer to the same dilemma:

If I am an employee in a large corporation, I want my messages nice and clean from the leadership down and if they don't do this, they are not doing a good job.

What that means is that the leaders cannot admit to any uncertainty about what I am talking about, I must have all the questions thought out. I cannot live with something unless it is thought out to the nth degree and I have answers to every single question that anyone could possibly have thought of.

This situation presents business leaders with a vicious cycle and this cycle is based on an infantalisation of the workforce and the perception that people cannot deal with ambiguity. Building a resilient organisation means building people who are comfortable with ambiguity, uncertainty and paradox.

What is required is navigational leadership – the capability to instil a collective sense of where the organisation is and the confidence and optimism to move forward into an uncertain future. It has four elements:

- inspiring confidence in the organisation in the context of its current state;
- ensuring transparency, accountability and good governance;
- encouraging speedy and informed decision-making;
- involving and engaging staff at all levels.

Defence technology manufacturer

To step into an uncertain future, managers need confidence and especially a sense of optimism. They have to believe they can make a difference, that they can help build a positive picture of the future. If they can't do this, if they can only be negative about the future, a sense of helplessness and paralysis sinks in. The business begins to feel it is a victim and that it cannot do anything positive to shape its future.

Learning and development manager

States of Jersey

By definition, you cannot know everything in uncertain environments – the days of Renaissance man are long gone. Management teams need to try to find individuals with different thinking paradigms who will challenge their assumptions and habitual thought patterns. These ideas must be grounded in some sort of evidence. The stuff of leadership is to recognise, ascribe value and integrate these new ideas in such a way that managers can act upon them. In a sense, it is the process of developing a narrative about the future, having a viable story that employees can believe and want to be a part of.

This is vitally important, especially for managers in a leadership role. Of course, leaders need to have a realistic sense of what they can achieve and of course they will have doubts at times. But even if you are frightened to death, you have to show the belief that the situation can be overturned and changed for the better. If you don't or can't demonstrate that belief, why should people follow you? Leaders have to be upbeat. People have to have something to follow, some vision or sense of possibility during times of uncertainty.

Chris Stephenson

Random House

I think optimism and confidence are absolutely crucial in leading people through difficult times. Yes, acknowledge the difficulty, acknowledge it is not all roses, but be confident. It is hugely important to show that you are confident that the business will be successful through this time, we will be the best we can be, we will be the best in the industry through this time. When people's heads go down, their performance goes down, so it is critical to remain confident. However, leaders must not be blind to the realities. Sometimes it can be all too easy to go the other way and assume we're fine, we'll always be fine and that attitude is quite dangerous.

You have to make sure a clear message is being passed down about the expectation that people will engage.

That is true for any form of difficult change, but in terms of uncertainty or chaos, it is like turning the volume up. In chaotic or uncertain times, it is easier to absent yourself because there is so much going on. It may be that people feel less certain themselves, or more stressed. That can lead to inaction, which then becomes mental absenteeism and absenteeism of leadership. It is important to be really clear and get commitment from everyone that we are one and this is the one voice that people internally and externally will hear. That creates the confidence and "positivity" that begins to permeate the organisation.

Neil Morrison

Inspiring confidence

A 2008 online survey of 125 managers together with some 40 interviews with senior leaders by Kevin Power and Andrew Day of the Ashridge Consulting Group highlighted the paralysing impact of fear of the unknown faced by organisations during periods of turbulence.[1] The research highlighted how many organisations experienced division, denial and fragmentation during that year. In some cases, leaders became detached from their staff, with the accompanying danger of the organisation failing to respond coherently to the challenges facing it.

Power and Day commented:

> At the centre of the leadership experience is the challenge of dealing with the uncertainty of the current environment. Perception is everything and this can change from day to day. So one day it feels like the business might be stabilising, then the next day new information could change this sense of hope back into a state of despair.
>
> Of course in some instances, the impact has been immediate and tangible. For certain sectors, such as the automotive industry and its supply chain, volumes have dropped by up to 40-60% in some cases.

The first and most immediate task of business leaders in these circumstances is therefore to inspire confidence and provide an accurate context of where the organisation is. The Ashridge report indicates the following priorities:

- making sense of the external environment;
- understanding where you are exposed and managing risk;
- making tough decisions and providing tough feedback about company performance;
- providing effective responses to changing conditions;
- helping people to understand how the context has changed.

The overwhelming priority cited by the business leaders interviewed for this book was the need for effective inspirational communication at all levels.

Ford Motor Company

Lessons learnt about surviving and thriving in turbulence – the business leadership and culture, not just at the top of the business but at every level, has got to get everyone believing and engaged. Communication is critical, so is seeing success. We need people to walk the talk so that people in five or ten years' time are still committed to the plan.

Neil Schloss

Honda Europe

For me [leadership] is about keeping that sense of direction and keeping the faith, in terms of "guys we can see our way through this, we know it is very difficult, it is uncertain but we still feel we are in the right direction – stick with us".

Ian Howells

Simmons & Simmons

Leadership behaviours are critical. One is that sense of optimism and confidence in what you're doing. The eyes of your firm will always be on you. What really differentiates an effective leader is not technical skill but the ability to talk about your vision of the future in a way that makes your people think, "wow, this is a great place to be", that makes them feel the company is going somewhere, that inspires people and generates trust and belief in the leadership.

Dan Flint

From those such as the people quoted above, a number of priorities emerge about the nature of communication during periods of intense uncertainty.

Nokia

We have multiple points of scorching heat that are fuelling a blazing fire around us. For example, there is intense heat coming from our competitors, more rapidly than we ever expected.

While competitors poured flames on our market share, what happened at Nokia? We fell behind, we missed big trends, and we lost time. At that time, we thought we were making the right decisions; but, with the benefit of hindsight, we now find ourselves years behind.

And the truly perplexing aspect is that we're not even fighting with the right weapons. We are still too often trying to approach each price range on a device-to-device basis.

In the meantime, we've lost market share, we've lost mind share and we've lost time.

How did we get to this point? Why did we fall behind when the world around us evolved?

This is what I have been trying to understand. I believe at least some of it has been due to our attitude inside Nokia. We poured gasoline on our own burning platform. I believe we have lacked accountability and leadership to align and direct the company through these disruptive times. We had a series of misses. We haven't been delivering innovation fast enough. We're not collaborating internally.

Nokia, our platform is burning.

Extracts from an internal memo, February 2009
Stephen Elop
Chief executive

Honesty

The communication should be honest. Disingenuous platitudes about the company's situation that are clearly at odds with what employees, clients, investors and other stakeholders are picking up from other sources will reinforce existing feelings of cynicism or fear. This may well lead to a haemorrhage of talent or passive apathy across the business just at a time when the organisation may need to move quickly and decisively.

Clarity

The communication should – in vivid terms that can be understood by everyone in the organisation – be clear about where the company stands. It should focus people's attention on the priorities and challenges facing the organisation, even if there is no immediate crisis to solve.

Inspirational

The communication should inspire confidence and faith in the ability of the organisation to steer its way through the uncertainty facing it. As Mark Thomas says:

You don't necessarily have to be sunny as a leader, you don't have to say it will be alright. It is perfectly possible as a leader to say "this will be a terrible time, all I have to offer is blood, sweat, toil and tears" and still have people follow you. There are examples of leaders who have said precisely that and have led very effectively.

What is necessary is that you have some sort of vision of what the shape of success will be and some idea of how the journey is going to look. The more you are able to paint that picture with vivid colours, the more likely you are to motivate people to follow you. The more you say "I don't know what the destination looks like", especially if you are really vague, and say "I don't know whether it is north or south I just know it is not here", the more difficult it is to motivate people.

Combining a high degree of uncertainty with a high degree of motivation is intrinsically difficult – but the ability to achieve it is the most important skill in managing uncertainty effectively.

Involving

The communication should make employees and other stakeholders feel involved and that they have a crucial and influential role to play,

The Cochrane Collaboration

The Cochrane Collaboration is a global health-care charity that conducts research through a network of 15,000 independent scientists and researchers. During 2008–09, the charity embarked upon a strategic review of its future. It conducted a global "conversation" with some 3,000 members which it believes has been highly successful in achieving large-scale engagement.

With a limited budget and a small team to undertake the review, the charity's steering committee decided to conduct it through e-mail, phone and shared e-documents. Supported by Ashridge consultants, the review team held "inquiry conversations" over six months with members at gatherings in Italy, India and the UK, and with external stakeholders such as academic and medical institutions. These revealed important challenges and concerns about the charity's future. The team identified seven "threads of conversation" on such themes as purpose, accountability and decision-making, financial viability, and external and internal coherence. These themes formed the basis of the dialogue about the charity's future.

Over a six-month period ending in spring 2009, more than 3,000 members joined the conversation through questionnaires, telephone discussions with the review team, debates at various

so that the sense of helplessness and apathy that often accompanies "the unknown" is dispelled.

Ensuring transparency, accountability, good governance

The incoming president of Luxfer Gas Cylinders transformed the execution of his strategy with a roadmap that provided clear and transparent criteria against which his senior management team could report their progress against goals (see Chapter 2).

Transparency, accountability and the resulting good governance are not only important in their own right. They are also critical in managing uncertainty because they:

international conferences and the Cochrane Colloquium, and visits to the charity's website.

The Cochrane Colloquium, an annual two-day event, played an important role, involving large numbers of members in the inquiry. There were presentations and discussions, and an exhibition area featuring storyboards from the inquiry to help give a flavour of the wide variety of ideas and perspectives contributed by members.

Jeremy Grimshaw, director of the Canadian Cochrane Centre and joint leader of the review team, says:[2]

I was extremely nervous going [to the Colloquium], but within 24 hours we knew that it was the right approach for our organisation. We got over the idea to participants that this was their review. They took responsibility for ensuring their voices were heard during the review and for taking forward actions resulting from the review.

For the Cochrane Collaboration participation is not democracy, and the steering committee retains responsibility for decisions about the charity's future. However, its decisions are influenced by the insights and ideas of over 3,000 members.

- ensure that goals, and the criteria against which they are set, are clearly understood and articulated, removing the possibility of misinterpretation and deviation by frontline staff;
- ensure that resources – money, technology, people – are properly allocated and not misused or siphoned off for pet projects that have little or nothing to do with an organisation's stated goals;
- allow large organisations with complex structures to respond quickly to sudden shifts in direction and to build up financial reserves that provide essential liquidity for use in unanticipated crises or opportunities (see Chapter 4).

Transparency, accountability and good governance are critical if an organisation is to have the capability and agility to change course and reallocate resources to cope with unexpected change and to take advantage of unforeseen opportunities.

Ford's dramatic turnaround in the years since Alan Mulally took over as president and chief executive in September 2006 is ascribed in part to the transparency of the financial reporting system he introduced to the company's strategic planning. Previously managers held "pre-meetings" before board meetings where they agreed on how to draw attention away from any poor performance and investment decisions. It was a classic "cover your ass" manoeuvre and antithetical to the kind of flexible and responsive problem-solving that Mulally wanted to introduce at a time when the company was facing a very uncertain future.

Mulally had seen this kind of thing before when he was running engineering at Boeing's commercial plane division. In 1997, Boeing took a $2.7 billion loss after a failure of communication in the commercial division led to two assembly lines being closed for a month at a time when demand was rising. When Mulally became CEO of the division in 1999, he kicked off a new era of radical transparency that made everyone better informed and much more aware of performance issues and potential problems.

He took that philosophy to Ford. As at Boeing, Mulally was determined to have a constant stream of data that would give his team a weekly snapshot of Ford's global operations and measure executives' performance against profit targets. Constantly updated numbers – later validated by pre-earnings quarterly audits – would make it impossible for executives to hide unpleasant truths. But that wasn't the only objective. "Information should never be used as a weapon on a team," says Mulally. Rather, the numbers would help executives anticipate problems and tweak strategy accordingly.

When Mulally first instituted the weekly business plan review system, it was viewed not only as a pain in the neck but, as one senior member of the management team commented, "it was also like playing poker with all your cards showing". However, the new system quickly proved itself and is now seen as a template of effective navigational leadership, as Ford's Neil Schloss explains:

Alan Mulally introduced the new reporting system in 2006. Events of 2008-09, when things were at rock bottom, showed us the proof of how well we executed decisions and whether the process worked. The weekly Thursday reviews were the way we had moved to transparency, openness and honesty – it hadn't been part of the Ford culture before Alan arrived. All our leaders were focused on their part of the business; we weren't looking at how to leverage our assets globally.

We were great at fixing problems, restructuring, etc, reacting to something that needed fixing, but we didn't share the learning across the business. Once we solved the problem, we got back to the job and didn't communicate across the business. There was no process in place, no learning, we would rehash the same problems and we certainly weren't leveraging our resources globally.

Alan came in, put in the new reporting process and institutionalised it. Previously, no one wanted to bring bad news to the executive meeting; then we began to see it was OK to deal with reality and to be transparent about problems and issues – what was not OK was to ignore the problems and not to deal with this. We were all great at dealing with problems, but now we could be open about this and be rewarded for this transparency, so buy-in was not difficult.

We saw the process working in the wake of the Japanese earthquake in 2011, which had such a critical impact on the suppliers of car manufacturers. The earthquake happened on Thursday and by Friday, we were able to hold our executive meeting and bring everyone together to look at how we could deal with the reality and the resulting problems.

We had all the usual heads across the global business, global business unit heads and divisional reps, including logistics, manufacturing, product development, HR, treasury, etc, all looking at the reality of what had happened and the resulting problems. The team met daily to look at what we knew and held "special attention meetings" to look at what's happening on the ground and how we could respond.

We didn't have any product stoppages and we're the only car manufacturer to have achieved this as far as I know. That whole

HSBC Rail (UK)

HSBC Rail, established in the late 1990s to meet the investment and financing requirements of the UK's passenger and freight rail industry, based its strategic reporting on a strategic map initiated by the company's chief executive, Peter Aldridge, and developed by Robert Kaplan and David Norton, inventors of the balanced scorecard.

One of Aldridge's most important goals was to make the organisation "more responsive on its feet" in a time of uncertainty. The strategic map helps do this by assessing and aligning each function's contribution to the business under four themes:

- Capital efficiency
- Customer relationship
- Operational excellence
- Learning and growth

An important principle was that the managers appointed to oversee each theme, the theme owners, had the data they needed to plot and describe progress to the management team on a regular basis. This ensured that the strategy map was the centrepiece of the company's business reporting framework.

In an interview in 2006, Aldridge concluded:[3]

> One of the most important changes we introduced was that members of the team do not spend the whole of the meeting reporting on financial issues such as the current return on equity. Rather, each theme owner highlights the objective on the map that they are currently focusing on and how the company is performing against them.
>
> Usually the discussion and debate are around the resources we are throwing at the objective. Have we got the right people at the right time in the right place? Does the theme owner need extra help? Have you been surprised by something and do we need to change it?

We always establish accountabilities and time frames: who is going to perform this or that task and when is it going to be undertaken by? This kind of review may be different from the strictly financial review we undertook in the past – but it is not undertaken any less rigorously.

A key objective of the HSBC Rail strategic map was to help the company be "more responsive on its feet" so that it could anticipate and respond effectively to uncertainty. An example of how this looked in the company's strategic plan is as follows.

Goal: to develop a responsive organisation
Key activities
- **Theme: capital efficiency**
  - Develop alternative capital and funding structures
- **Theme: customer relationship management**
  - Work proactively with operators to build strong relationships and develop value-added solutions
  - Build a strong relationship with the Department of Transport and other government bodies and third-party investors
  - Build market intelligence that positions us to be the supplier of choice for the right deals
- **Theme: operational excellence**
  - Deliver highly effective, customer-focused supplier performance
  - Continue to invest resources selectively to minimise our residual value risk
  - Focus on business process excellence to deliver improvement in productivity
- **Theme: learning and growth**
  - Share and implement best practices

communication link didn't exist prior to 2006 when Alan introduced the process. I'm convinced that we've responded to Japan so effectively because our meeting process enables all the perspectives across the business to come together to help us respond – essentially this process has become our enterprise risk management process.

Before 2006, we had gone through many difficult problems, but I would say that 75% of the reason why we were able to transform ourselves through the new meeting process was because of Alan's leadership – he was able to come in and transform the business.

This hasn't entailed a new executive team; the leadership team is pretty much the same as the one that Alan took over in 2006. He got buy-in to the reporting process pretty quickly. From a personal point of view, I was sceptical of a new leader and a new reporting process, but it made logical sense. We had to get over the fear of being transparent.

Encouraging speedy and well-informed decision-making

A transparent and full accountable reporting system also supports informed and innovative decision-making – the third important priority of the leadership required in managing uncertainty.

The first facet of effective decision-making in uncertain times is speed. The two most telling findings of the managing uncertainty survey were that the majority of the companies surveyed failed to respond quickly enough to the early signals of the 2008 crisis, and that those that felt they made the right decisions were also those that responded faster.

As was highlighted in Chapter 2, one of the most important reasons respondents advocated the better integration of strategy formulation and execution is the speed that is necessary to exploit opportunities in an uncertain environment.

If the need for speed is the primary factor in making decisions in an uncertain environment, then the need for diversity – not just in the ethnic origins and sex of the workforce but also in their skills, outlook, perspective, attitude and thinking – is a close second. Phiroz Bhagat, author of *Pattern Recognition in Industry* (see Chapter 2) argues that when executives cite "gut instinct" as a key factor in

---

Marsh

*The first thing we needed [in response to the crisis of 2008] was
quick recognition that the crisis was upon us and that this was
not a storm in a teacup in a mid-quarter. We reacted within the
first two quarters but nevertheless we feel that it could have been
faster.*

*Second, we recognised that this was not a temporary crash
but a longer-term issue and therefore our plan for a shorter-term
crisis would have to be revised. We were slow in developing a
strategic plan that dealt with a longer-term crisis.*

*We ran scenarios of maximum conceivable loss for our
clients but did not apply them to ourselves in terms of the worst
possible scenario. It was a matter of creating financial buffers or
reserves to cover an error in our planning. That was the main
lesson for us – you have to create those buffers and you need
speedy analysis to spot when you need to use them.*

Daniel Galvao

---

effective decision-making, what they are in fact relying on is "a set
of internalised mental models" that shape their interpretation of the
information in front of them.

It follows that a lack of diversity in the senior management team
will bring with it the danger of undue orthodoxy in the way the team
thinks through strategic challenges and solutions.

As a senior executive at one of Europe's leading technology firms
explains:

*We do not currently have the capability to expand into new markets
and this is the basis of the uncertainty now facing us. Future
expansion will require a different set of skills and a different way of
managing and developing the business. We don't know how to do it.*

*We don't know what the future skill set will be and this is a
big problem. The future involves risk and a new definition of the
business. We will need a strongly collaborative mindset across the*

business – no one operating company can do it alone, we need to be together. We are far away from this mindset. All the different country operations want to do things their own way, particularly the US business which we acquired relatively recently and which is proving hostile and unco-operative.

A big problem for me is that our board directors are all white, male, of similar age and professional experience, with engineering backgrounds. This similarity is not helpful when we are moving towards such uncertainty. The more diverse our company, and particularly our executive team, the more likely we will be innovative, which is what we need to help us through uncertainty and change.

The importance of ensuring that there is a diverse set of perspectives when making strategic decisions was explored in a survey of senior executives by Henley Management College in 2009.[4] The resulting report concluded:

Decision-makers face an increasing range of apparently contradictory priorities.

First, the world is more connected: with more than 1 billion web users, more information is available to support and challenge any given point of view. Second, the burgeoning use of "blogs" and other networked forms of social activities create pressure for significant decisions to satisfy the values of many more stakeholders: NGOs, shareholders and local residents have more opportunity to garner broad support to stand against single interest decisions.

Third, the accelerating rate of change in business and civil society compared with the plodding pace of government, law, education and politics often means priorities in these two different spheres are unsynchronised. Combine these contradictory priorities with the lessening constraints of geographical boundaries, and the challenges of strategic decision-making become extremely demanding.

When attention is scarce, people categorise incoming evidence and information into familiar frames of reference, to delineate the problem space. Narrow framing leads to inappropriate decisions with unintended consequences ... American government

Capital One Bank

Capital One Bank's ability to wrest opportunity from crisis, particularly in the acquisition of Chevy Chase Bank in 2008, was derived, in part, from the senior executive team's ability to sift and interpret market analysis from independent experts, strategic partners and suppliers. Iain Worsley elaborates:

At the time of the 2008 crisis, we were in the middle of a restructure in the way we covered our clients so we had engaged various consulting groups which promoted best practice. Equally, we had our own internal economists who were able to provide information and data. Again, we talked to counterparts in the marketplace and our clients to get a flow of information from them as well. We talk to other banks on a regular basis to find out what issues they are confronting.

studies suggest that most major intelligence failures are caused by discounting, misinterpreting, ignoring or rejecting relevant information that does not fit the prevailing mental model. Yet managers are expected to make sense of situations convincingly.

The Henley survey confirms how crucial the effective interpretation of the information available to senior executives is in decision-making. But in some, if not many, cases this is merely a matter of the good use of analytical skills (see Chapter 6 for a more detailed exploration of effective analytics).

But what do senior decision-makers do when the information they require to make their decisions is unavailable, incomplete or ambiguous? Companies in the managing uncertainty survey such as Honda Europe, Random House, Capital One Bank, Balfour Beatty and RBS now make a point of helping managers through the use of option evaluation, pattern recognition and scenario planning to take decisions despite seemingly inadequate, confusing or conflicting data.

All these approaches are helpful, but as the Henley survey stresses, it is crucial to update and adjust constantly not just the accuracy and

RBS

There are external factors that you just cannot predict. I think that there are a number of categories where ambiguity and judgment are not necessarily things that you can codify on a computer or an inventory that takes all of that away.

What you can do is to try and make sure that your data is as accurate and up-to-date as you can make it. You capture the knowledge of other individuals who have dealt with other scenarios that may not be identical but, assembled together, will enable you to discern common patterns. There are people in this organisation who are around today who were also around during the last economic recession. We are starting to use knowledge-management tools to enable us to help codify that as well. There are models and tools you can adopt to teach people that you live in a world that is volatile and not entirely in your control.

We introduced collaboration tools in partnership with Accenture. We were offshoring some technology about operations and we were concerned that we would lose some of the knowledge. It was initially used to ensure we did not lose the technology knowledge but it has been expanded so that we can use connections to bridge the gap between user groups and communities concerned with the topic. There are also knowledge repository tools in specific areas.

If there are new regulatory risks emerging, our risk management academy, owned by our risk management experts, can post training materials or organise seminars.

Donna Hamilton

relevance of the data available to strategic decision-makers but also the mental models (in the form of assumptions and "givens") being used to interpret this data. The Henley report made the following observations linked to how the human brain works:[5]

The sense-making process focuses attention on what is important by sifting and filtering input through a "pre-organised mechanism" of "noticing and bracketing" – distinguishing similarities and differences and making connections between them. This process evolved to increase the chances of survival by triggering fast, relatively instinctive responses to stimuli which experience suggests are "good or bad" for the individual.

Over time, the brain develops "well trodden" neural pathways, which represent meaningful aggregations of categories, that is, conceptual interpretations. However, when faced with novel and unpredictable situations, this quick and economical sense-making process has several limitations.

First, the neural pathways to cognitive reasoning pass through the emotional centres, so that "we feel before we think". In fact we cannot make decisions without emotions, they enable us to prioritise alternatives. Unfortunately, nature's approach tends to force attention on the negative outcomes to which a given action might lead, to protect against future losses and allow us to choose among fewer alternatives.

In some people the urge to avoid risk is stronger than in others, but the point here is that both risk and uncertainty tend to create anxiety, and decision-makers may try to eliminate this discomfort by categorising circumstances too quickly. This immediately filters what is noticed, often quite unconsciously.

Stereotypes, preconceptions and well-established preferences further limit what is noticed. The more experience a person has the more they are able to provide quick and plausible explanations for combinations of circumstances.

Unfortunately, in complex situations with many interconnected variables, it is often the small details at the periphery, the weak signals that radically affect how a scenario plays out.

These are the least likely factors to figure in the framing of an experienced manager trained to pay attention to what resonates with their historical success.

The ability to frame decisions in the right context and ensure that decision-making at all levels is informed by a diverse but consensual understanding of the priorities facing the organisation is paramount. This requires clear leadership.

Involving and engaging staff

Chapter 2 looked at how strategy formulation and execution need to be integrated if goals are to be met and the organisation is to be able to respond more quickly to unexpected events. This cannot be done without the involvement and engagement of employees at all levels.

To achieve bottom-up engagement and innovative decision-making at all levels, companies like Diageo, Pfizer, Domaine Chandon and East African Breweries are experimenting with "mission leadership", an approach lifted directly from command philosophies adopted by the American and British armed forces.

Mission command is an approach, in its military form, which promotes decentralised action, freedom and speed of execution. It has the following elements:

- a commander gives orders in a manner that ensures subordinates understand his intentions, their own missions and the context of those missions;
- subordinates are told the effect they are to achieve and the reason it needs to be achieved;
- subordinates are given the resources they need to carry out their missions;
- the commander uses the minimum control measures (so as not to limit the freedom of action of subordinates);
- subordinates then decide (within their delegated freedom) how best to achieve their mission – put more simply, "tell me what to do, not how to do it".

Mission leadership helped Pfizer resolve the widespread cynicism and the "them and us" mentality that existed among its R&D teams a decade or so ago.

David Roblin, Pfizer's former head of clinical R&D, recognised that cynics are often frustrated idealists and that if the significant resources and expertise of the organisation could be properly aligned with the specific needs of the project teams, and be seen to do so, a turnaround in attitudes and behaviour could be dramatic.

Two problems in particular were high on Roblin's list. The first was the need for clarity. As he explains:

> Getting people to sit down and go through the intellectual articulation of a simple mission is more problematic than it initially seems. Many people think they have done it when in fact they haven't. For example, there is no point in setting tight deadlines for a research project to have reached a certain point in the clinical or regulatory process if the purpose of the exercise is first to question whether the market wants it. That is putting the cart before the horse.
>
> Getting this right requires the heads of line to be very clear from the outset about what the mission is, and to pause sufficiently in the consultation to ensure awareness and understanding. It then requires clinical research staff on the projects to make very clear in the way they draw up clearly articulated statements of what they need to do the job.
>
> To achieve this, we decided to review the way we consulted and communicated. We found, for example, that the large project meetings we were holding every week were very good for achieving the right alignment between the project's main mission and the goals of the organisation. However, they were not a good forum for detailed planning and the process of breaking down decisions into sub-missions.
>
> The various components of a large multidisciplinary clinical research team – pharmaceutical scientists, regulatory experts, manufacturing experts – all needed to talk to each other on a regular basis. Much smaller groups were needed to achieve this.

The second was the need for empowerment – in this case, the empowerment that would emerge when, having established a clear idea of the main mission, staff of clinical research teams felt able to harness the resources of the organisation behind it and explore innovative ways to keep the project on track.

Roblin wanted to demonstrate to scientific and technical staff that the "system" would work for them if it was creatively challenged:

Random House

Agility comes down to a couple of things. One is collective leadership. We have talked a lot within the board that if you don't know or can't totally forecast what will happen, then if something does hit suddenly, you want the business to jump in one direction instead of scattering. If people scatter, it takes a long time to get everyone back together, focused and moving in the same direction.

Neil Morrison

Wipro Infocrossing

Whatever actions the company takes, we always try to encourage a bottom-up approach which allows staff to influence the decisions. Getting the employees on the same plain as senior management was a priority, particularly in terms of pinpointing what was happening in the external world.

We encourage employees to participate in a quarterly communication exercise and in some cases we have increased the regularity to monthly meetings. These have proved highly successful, not only in keeping us abreast of new and emerging

Often their sense that the system was working against them was based on untried and untested assumptions. I threw out a challenge to one team that if it could identify the barriers that were being placed in its path, I'd personally remove them. On investigation they found that most of the procedures or processes that they saw as obstructive were precedents set by previous teams rather than by management. In the end, the only thing they wanted was to change a policy on the ability to order sandwiches out of hours.

Colin Ewen, a project leader, emphasises the role mission leadership played in enabling the company to convince people of the importance of R&D and its strategic intent in conducting it:

trends but also in communicating to employees where we are in the crisis. It is very important that we are open and honest with them so that they are made part of the solution.

Shivakumar Rajagopalin

SunGard India

As somebody who has been managing a number of businesses, I feel my job has always been to set the goal and then get out of the way. Middle managers and employees are much better qualified to deal with the problems.

We can at best set the direction for the business and reduce the complexity so managers and staff understand how they can deal with it but we must then move out of the way. Too often managers are forced to spend enormous amounts of time managing upwards – and this directly contributes to lack of speed.

Praful Pillay

It enabled us to establish the strategic objective clearly in people's heads in advance, reach a strategic agreement on objectives and review progress against the original plan.

But the real benefit, he stresses, mirroring Roblin's conclusions, was the freedom it granted team members to follow their instincts and ideas on how to achieve their objectives – so long as this supported the project's main mission:

Previously there had been reluctance among staff to explore this freedom. There was a worry that some gung-ho project leader would place them in an awkward position that would have repercussions when their performance was reviewed and appraised at the end of the year by their heads of lines. They never explored the boundaries

---

> ## Balfour Beatty
>
> *This business has relatively free decision-making capabilities, so giving people the confidence to make decisions is at the heart of what we are trying to do operationally.*
>
> *The problem is that in a time of crisis, there is a bit of an impasse as people are looking for guidance much more. This can slow down your decision-making. However, empowering people to get on with it and to operate in a way that they think is commercially sound in their area of the business has helped us.*
>
> *The disadvantage is that it can be a locally driven agenda, but the advantage is that it consists of lots of little decisions that are largely made in conjunction with the client rather than big strategic decisions where you can get it wrong.*
>
> *We have always been quite decentralised, but getting people to make decisions and lead in their markets is something we are looking for more of. It's our business model for getting out of this current downturn. If we make our staff more mobile, that will grow our business and they will get the right people into the right positions in the business and they can make the decisions that will make the difference.*
>
> Richard Gartside

because they did not feel they had been given the licence to do so. I gave them that licence. I told them that they could do anything as long as it is not illegal, involves fraud or contravenes government regulations.

Conclusion

Whether senior executives use mission leadership or some other form of delegation, staff empowerment is critical in helping organisations respond to uncertainty. It enables businesses to respond quickly to unexpected threats or opportunities, fostering innovation in products, services and management methods. It also ensures that strategic goals are adhered to while leaving middle and junior managers as well as frontline technical staff free to use their own knowledge and skills to reach these goals – and in the process everyone acquires a sense of ownership of the "solutions" that are developed.

4 Agility

The capability to move rapidly and flexibly in order to shape or adapt to the opportunities or threats arising from uncertainty

> *Build your capability to respond. Do this quickly, in terms of the right processes and systems so that when the next shock comes around and a new area of uncertainty comes up, you're ready. Or if it is a prolonged period of uncertainty then you have the systems and processes in place to allow you to respond to that period.*
>
> Ian Howells, Honda Europe

THE EXPERIENCE OF CRISIS and prolonged uncertainty has given new life and urgency to the notion of agility for many international businesses. Many of the companies that took part in the managing uncertainty survey carried out for this book are working on how they can become better able to respond quickly and flexibly to unexpected change and surprising events, and more adept at shaping events to their advantage. Up to now, when faced with a changing, uncertain and potentially volatile operating environment, some companies have simply stood by, waiting for trends to become clearer, while some have been taken unawares by a threat that has emerged from the fog of uncertainty. Others, however, have focused on processes and structures that enable them to act nimbly in response to change and to take advantage of unexpected opportunities.

Fleet of foot

Much has been written about agility as a trait of innovative companies that succeed through bold competitive moves. Apple is

---

Random House

As a board, we have talked a lot about uncertain times and how, when you can't forecast the future, you then have to look at the organisational ability to manage in these circumstances. It changes from a skill set that is based on knowing where we are going, knowing our environment and therefore looking to maximise our return in this stable environment, to a place where we have to focus on being able to react very quickly.

We could forever be pondering how things will be and getting it wrong. What we can do is to manage our organisation in a way that makes it agile.

Neil Morrison

---

seen as "king" of agile because of its devastating ability to launch innovative products that have wrong-footed rivals and transformed the market overnight.

Agile companies like Amazon and Apple have recognised or created a source of advantage and exploited it quickly and ruthlessly. Speed of movement is unarguably one demonstration of agility, as is the ability to exploit new or disruptive technologies. These companies lead rather than respond, and indeed their surprising actions trigger uncertainty for less innovative rivals.

It is easy to assume that agility is the preserve of innovative market leaders in fast-moving industries. But such an assumption is dangerous and untrue when companies are operating in unpredictable conditions. Survival and long-term success depend on the ability to move fast, either defensively or opportunistically, as soon as there is a brief glimpse through the fog of uncertainty.

New rules

The ability to change "the rules of the game" is another trait of agility, an example of which is Google's rapid dominance of the smartphone market through its Android operating system. Based on open-source software, Google has successfully created a new "eco system" to rival Apple's. Approximately 28 handset operators now use the Android operating system.

In a leaked memo to employees in February 2011, Stephen Elop, chief executive of Nokia, ruefully described the rapidity of Android's success:[1]

> In about two years, Android created a platform that attracts application developers, service providers and hardware manufacturers. Android came in at the high end, they are now winning the mid-range, and quickly they are going downstream to phones under £100. Google has become a gravitational force, drawing much of the industry's innovation to its core.

Nokia saw its market value fall from a high of €151 billion at the end of 2007 to €15 billion in early 2011 and knew it had to change strategic direction. In April 2011 it announced an alliance with Microsoft that will entail Nokia gradually phasing out its own software and adopting the Windows operating system for all its high-end handsets. But whether they can ever now compete with Android and Apple phones is questionable. Nokia may simply have left it too late in responding to the almost seismic shift in its market. The signs so far are not encouraging – by June 2012, after Nokia announced that losses from its mobile-phone business were larger than expected, its market value fell to its lowest level for 16 years to €8.3 billion; its share price dipped below €2 for the first time since 1996.

Provided they have the capability to identify opportunities, agile companies are much better placed to move into a competitive space overlooked by rivals. MediaTek, a Taiwanese company that makes mobile-phone chips, recognised the potential of China's nascent phone-manufacturing market. The company focused on producing cheap second-generation mobile-phone chips for the new Chinese phonemakers, while Western rivals scrambled to develop third-generation (3G) chips for use in smartphones. The Chinese phonemakers are rapidly moving upmarket and are now challenging leading top-tier brands in many emerging markets. They are also shifting towards smartphones, and MediaTek has responded by developing a smartphone chip that uses the Android operating system.

Competing through agility

The ability to change direction and move rapidly in uncertain conditions is critical. Extensive research conducted by McKinsey shows a correlation between agility and successful performance in turbulent markets. (McKinsey defines agility as "the capacity to identify and capture opportunities more quickly than rivals do" and turbulence as "a measure of the frequency of unpredictable changes affecting the ability of companies to create and sustain value".)[2]

An international survey of executives by McKinsey in 2006, for example, suggested the benefits of agility to be higher revenues, more satisfied customers and employees, improved operational efficiencies and a faster time to market. Nine out of ten executives ranked agility both as critical to business success and as growing in importance over time.[3]

The crucial advantage agile firms have is highlighted by Donald Sull, who led the research at McKinsey and is professor of management practice in strategic and international management at London Business School:

> In turbulent markets, agility is invaluable. When the cumulative effect of uncertainty gets bigger and bigger, you get some great opportunities out there. You need to attack those opportunities. Managers need to be entrepreneurial and aggressive, willing to take risks, mobilise resources, adapt to circumstances and live with uncertainty.

More recent research in 2009 by the Economist Intelligence Unit echoes this message.[4] Based on the responses of 349 executives around the world, the findings revealed that:

- some 27% of respondents said their organisation is at a competitive disadvantage because it is not agile enough to anticipate fundamental market shifts;

■ nearly 90% said that organisational agility is critical for business success;

■ half of all responding chief executives and chief information officers agreed that rapid decision-making and execution are essential for a company's competitive standing.

The Economist Intelligence Unit research also reveals that because of internal barriers it is not that easy for a firm to become more agile even if it tries to. More than 80% of respondents had taken action to improve agility, yet 34% said they had failed to deliver the desired benefits. The major barriers were slow decision-making, conflicting departmental goals and priorities, risk-adverse cultures and silo-based information.

A 2009 study of agility by London Business School and others involving 59 UK service organisations tried to establish a link between performance and agility.[5] The study revealed that only 22% of the responding organisations could be judged as agile and that these organisations enjoyed higher productivity, sales growth and customer satisfaction. It measured agility in two ways: the ability to respond to externally induced change; and the capability to excel simultaneously against a set of service performance indicators that enabled an organisation to "rapidly realign itself to meet changed customer demands".

The managing uncertainty survey revealed that the best-performing businesses moved quickly and flexibly to seize the advantage during this prolonged period of economic uncertainty and crisis. Most notably:

■ They were the quickest to take action – although even the quickest to act still took four months.

■ Those that responded faster were more satisfied with their decisions, despite having had less time to make them.

■ They consciously strove to increase their flexibility and responsiveness by:
   - improving operational efficiencies;
   - focusing on the profitable core of the business;

- making only moderate cost reductions (those firms that either undertook little or major cost cuts performed worse);
- preserving staff – staffing cuts correlated with poor performance;
- buying new businesses;
- avoiding fire sales of businesses at the lowest point of the business cycle.

■ They placed more importance on competitive awareness – those that believed they made the right decisions tended to be aware of and responsive to their rivals' actions.

■ They viewed the crisis as an opportunity rather than a threat – but only one-third of the respondents took this perspective.

As well as being asked about their experiences of the uncertainty caused by the economic crisis, the respondents were also asked how they intended to position themselves to meet the challenges ahead. What would be their most important actions for responding to future uncertainty?

The results suggest that companies are placing a higher priority on the actions that will strengthen their ability to respond swiftly to market opportunity. For instance, respondents indicate they will focus on the profitable core of their business and will also look harder for opportunities to cut costs and improve operational efficiencies.

Table 4.1 shows how companies are attaching greater importance to becoming more customer and market focused, more flexible and more innovation and growth oriented.

To explore these findings further, those interviewed in the follow-up to the survey were asked about their experiences and what they had learned during this period of prolonged uncertainty. Their responses highlighted four areas where their organisations were trying to become better equipped to deal with prolonged uncertainty:

■ financial agility;

■ operational agility;

■ portfolio agility;

■ organisational agility.

TABLE 4.1 **Present and future responses to crisis (%)**

	Response to the crisis	Future response to uncertainty
Investing in growth	47	74
Forging stronger and closer customer relationships	61	79
Flexible strategic planning	55	74
Developing innovative products and services	46	71
Targeting new markets and customers	48	70
Building capability and recruiting/developing talent	46	77
Empowering, enabling and mobilising staff	54	73

Source: © PA Knowledge 2011

Financial agility

The importance of liquidity

The credit crunch brought home the rude truth that without liquidity it is hard for businesses to thrive, even survive. Liquidity is an immensely reassuring buffer in uncertain and volatile times. Furthermore, when other businesses are struggling, the cash-rich, agile firm has a great competitive advantage. Cash-rich firms can exploit the opportunities that arise in economic downturns. They can buy ailing rivals or launch new products or expand into new markets overseas.

The survey highlighted the importance of liquidity in helping firms get through an economic downturn and also in enabling them to "respond as a winner". Mark Thomas of PA (who is also the author of *The Zombie Economy*, which looks at the challenges firms face when economic conditions are stagnant) believes that "capital will become a competitive weapon" as the global economy moves through a difficult economic transition, where uncertainty prevails. He comments:

> We are in a period of exceptional volatility in asset prices – notably share prices – and those who have access to capital, even as prices

tumble, can expect to make abnormal returns ... In this environment, highly liquid and well prepared companies can act opportunistically and make years' worth of progress almost overnight.

Many of the executives interviewed for this book stressed the importance of liquidity, especially those who had seen market conditions quickly deteriorate. Daniel Galvao, chief commercial officer and senior vice-president at Marsh, an insurance broker and risk adviser, describes how his company now gives much more thought to what he calls "financial buffers":

Liquidity is vital ... Operational risk can turn into financial risk very quickly. The economic crisis taught us that we need to create financial buffers to enable us to respond more effectively to unexpected events. We learned how to save for a rainy day. The reality is that without liquidity there is little chance of developing an effective response in the medium term as well as the long term.

For Ford, liquidity is an important plank in its strategy for recovery and growth. Forced to formulate a recovery plan in 2006 under the aegis of a new chief executive, Alan Mulally, the car manufacturer took the decision to maximise its liquidity, not just re-service its near crippling debt. This focus on liquidity proved a pivotal decision – and one that probably saved the business from following the path of General Motors and Chrysler, both of which were strapped for cash and forced to file for bankruptcy in 2009. Neil Schloss, Ford's treasurer and vice-president, comments:

Our experiences in 2006 and 2009 taught us that debt wouldn't bring us down, but a lack of liquidity would. Our decision in 2006 to raise cash was absolutely right. They say you can be lucky or good, but we were both lucky and good – we got it right, the new reporting process delivered the right set of decisions. We were looking for an $18 billion equity loan but we had a sense the markets are open today, we need to plan for uncertainty in the future, let's take advantage of the markets, let's go for $23.5 billion.

Lewis Booth, Ford's chief financial officer, confirmed the importance of liquidity in managing uncertainty:

When going into turbulent times, having enough liquidity is key and you need to have it before you need it. We saw commodity prices sharply increase and financial markets collapse. Auto industry volume fell sharply in the US and softened globally. We navigated through by having enough liquidity.

In some cases, this allowed us to turn the crisis into an opportunity. We continued to invest heavily in new products, even in the darkest of times. The liquidity we raised at the end of 2006 enabled us to not just refinance our debt but fund our restructuring plan and product investment, and protect for unforeseen events.

In most sectors, according to Thomas's research into "zombie economies" (which provides a sector by sector analysis), there are significant numbers of companies whose liquidity is in doubt. In *The Zombie Economy*, he predicts that these companies will suffer and many will not survive. Weakened competitors will see their share prices fall to levels that make them attractive acquisition targets. They may be forced to sell their most prized assets or "crown jewels" to raise cash. They may simply cease trading. Thomas says:

High-quality assets will become available – for anyone with the capital, and the courage, to acquire them – at bargain basement prices. Well-positioned companies can achieve a decade's worth of progress in two years.

PA's advice is to maximise liquidity – even at high cost. It recommends that companies rebuild their liquidity by taking the following steps:

- **Raising capital.** Organisations like Rio Tinto, TomTom and GKN have all raised significant sums through the equity markets.
- **Refinancing debt.** Some companies, like Yell and Schaeffler, have rolled over billions in bank finance. However, many businesses are still finding banks reluctant to lend and have turned to bond issuance as an alternative.
- **Divestment.** Companies can sell off valuable assets, such as Barclays did with Barclays Global Investors, and it is always better to do so before a crisis; otherwise it will be seen for the

fire sale it is and the price will be a fire-sale price. Furthermore, any sell-off that weakens a firm's core capability or its long-term competitive position may also shorten its life.

Cut costs but not capability

The managing uncertainty survey revealed that the most common action that companies took when the financial crisis struck was to cut costs. Some 82% of respondents cut costs. When asked about their future responses to uncertainty, 76% indicated they would continue to focus on cost reduction.

Thomas's research into the zombie economy reveals that cost cutting "to some degree is almost universal". Many businesses have now undertaken cost and capital reductions ranging from "a light touch approach to major surgery". These include:

- reducing travel and expenses;
- controlling discretionary spending;
- destocking;
- head-count reductions;
- hiring freezes;
- outsourcing back-office functions;
- plant relocations and closures.

For some companies, being the lowest-cost player in their market is a competitive strategy to gain market share. It is a strategy that has worked spectacularly well for companies from emerging markets, such as Tata and Kia Motors, South Korea's second largest automobile manufacturer.

Mindray, which manufactures medical equipment, has developed monitors that are priced at 10% of those produced by its Western competitors. SAB Miller, a South African brewer, outmanoeuvred its rivals by creating a low-cost beer based on a local crop that replaces expensively imported malt. A number of Indian businesses such as Tata Consultancy Services and Infosys have transformed the IT sector by carrying out increasingly skilled activities offshore at significantly lower cost.

Other companies resort to cost reduction as a defensive measure. Cost cutting will, of course, help to preserve profit in the short term and act as a buffer against unexpected market shocks. Evidence of a cost-effective structure helps keep analysts and shareholders on board and makes a business less vulnerable to predators.

However, a finding of the survey is that more successful firms made moderate and focused cuts. PA's analysis warns: "Cost cutting is helpful to total shareholder return but too much of it can be a bad thing because it damages long-term competitiveness".

Several of those interviewed in the survey follow-up stressed this message. Nick Laird, chief commercial officer at Ceridian, says flexibility and long-term profitability should be the priority:

By cutting costs, there is a danger you are also cutting capability. To be flexible to the customer, when you are pretty sure that next year the customer is going to need to draw on that capability, you need to stress that short-term cost cutting will damage long-term profitability. When we are cutting costs in our own team, we examine very carefully how flexible this will leave the organisation.

PA's analysis emphasises the importance of a "good" approach to cost cutting, which is to focus on:

- uncompetitive business, products or markets which are unlikely to create value (because the returns are below the cost of capital);
- non-core activities, projects or functions which are not essential for business sustainability or highly valued by customers.

In contrast, a "bad" approach is:
- indiscriminate – costs are targeted based on a category of spend, rather than whether they are creating value;
- damaging to long-term capacity or competitiveness;
- damaging to the company's ability to deliver high-quality products or service.

The rub is that cost cutting must be focused on not diminishing a business's ability to create value in the medium to long term. In one respect, this means not diminishing organisational agility.

RBS

All RBS's senior executives and senior managers have taken part in a programme of strategic value creation. This was in response to a serious concern that in an effort to respond to the crisis of recent years, we would implement short-term temporary cuts and changes that would cause long-term damage.

We had invested a lot of time in recruiting and developing senior executives. We introduced the concept of red and blue line thinking, pioneered by Kevin Kaiser and David Young of INSEAD, which discouraged people from advocating short-term temporary cuts in response to the immediate crisis without thinking about what the long-term impact might be in terms of value creation.

It was really about getting our executives to take a step back and think about the bigger picture – and we called it "thoughtful execution".

Donna Hamilton

Adopting a value-based focus

How can companies become more focused on creating value, especially in uncertain conditions? Two professors at INSEAD, Kevin Kaiser and David Young, are advocating a value-based focus which they call "blue line management".[6]

Kaiser and Young argue that companies mistakenly equate share price, earnings or market share with value (that is, where the expected value of cash coming into the business exceeds the amount going out), and that in reality, these aspects of business performance are simply indicators of value.

The problem is that many companies focus on these indicators, especially share price, which Kaiser and Young describe as "red line management". In doing so, they resort to "red line behaviour" where the priority is often to "finesse" their share price. This results in decisions and actions that can damage the real drivers of value creation.

Toyota is a business that allowed its attention to be diverted away from value creation towards market share. "Top managers became seduced by the idea of becoming the world's largest auto producer," say Kaiser and Young. In doing so, Toyota lost sight of safety and reliability. This resulted in a damaging wave of management errors and product recalls. The answer is to adopt "blue line management", which focuses on value creation over the long term as the overarching aim of a firm. This requires strategies and actions that maximise the drivers of value. These could include:

- shortening product development cycles;
- optimising inventory;
- learning from failure;
- strengthening team orientation;
- managing product quality;
- motivating employees;
- attention to customers.

Focusing on value creation plainly makes sense for companies that need to navigate through short-term turbulence while still building long-term sustainability. But how do they gain an accurate, "real-time" sense of the drivers of value creation when the environment is so volatile and company performance is being affected by many different variables, some of which are not even possible to identify?

Kaiser and Young acknowledge that this complexity inevitably results in "ignorance and uncertainty" but it is still possible for managers to manage through this. They argue:[7]

> Moving to a value-based culture requires everyone in the business to be continuously learning. Value creation demands experimentation ... Only through trial and error and, yes, failure, will managers gather new, relevant information to help them better understand the business and how they will get more value from it.

Understanding how the business creates value and inculcating value-driven processes and culture will help managers take better decisions about short-term cuts, and ensure that their business

Simmons & Simmons

A focus on cost is important, but it cannot be the be all and end all during uncertain conditions. You have to position yourself for growth. The thing you can do something about and which is in your control is to focus on your clients and really identify their needs.

The other thing you can do is to recognise the massive structural changes that are currently taking place in so many sectors. You have to ask yourself: "What are we going to do differently?" Doing nothing is not an option. You can't assume the same clients are going to come to you with the same requests or that you can go to them with the same offerings. You've got to change the way you operate and that requires a focus on innovation.

Dan Flint

has sufficient liquidity to build competitive advantage and seize opportunities that arise or are identified. But equally important in bolstering the liquidity that gives a business the financial agility to grow is a willingness to experiment and innovate.

Operational agility

Organisations have been compelled to rethink how they operate. Many are taking a fresh look at their organisational structure and processes to make sure they are fit for purpose in uncertain conditions.

Operational agility depends on how lean and flexible an organisation is. Processes must be as efficient as possible. Business units must be tightly aligned with their market and how it is developing so that they can respond quickly to geographical, demographic and segmental shifts as well as changing customer tastes and needs. The more flexible and adaptive an organisation is the more agile it will be.

Donald Sull of London Business School makes the point that operational agility is "not about a big strategic play, it's about a lot of small steps. It's about a firm's ability to exploit both revenue enhancing and cost cutting opportunities within its core business more quickly, effectively, and consistently than rivals do". He points to firms like easyJet, Tesco and Toyota ("even despite its recent woes") as "firms that have excelled at this type of operational agility. Over long periods of time, that can be really important".

Those interviewed in the follow-up to the managing uncertainty survey spoke of the need to be more flexible and fast moving, but they struggled to produce examples of how they have responded to this challenge. But the evidence is that operational agility is about balancing operational focus and efficiency with operational flexibility:

- **Operational focus** entails protecting and enhancing the profitable core through, for example, more efficient processes that add value or increase competitive advantage.
- **Operational flexibility** entails exploring medium-term and long-term growth opportunities and engaging in activities such as scenario planning.

The survey results underline the importance of a strong operational focus: 84% of respondents said their highest priority during the crisis was to improve operational efficiencies, and 91% said it would remain a priority in future.

Many of those interviewed mentioned speed of process as a "given" in their attempts to become more responsive. To increase its operational agility, Ford has aggressively restructured to improve profitability and maximise liquidity. It has also identified its product pipeline as one of its four main priorities. One aim is to accelerate the development of new products, especially battery electric vehicles (BEV) and plug-in hybrid electric vehicles (PHEV). Ford believes it has managed to speed up its product development process through a much more transparent weekly reporting system and by breaking down functional barriers to encourage learning across the global business.

Procter & Gamble has used modelling and simulation through virtual reality to reduce development costs and time to market. In a room full of high-resolution screens that create a three-dimensional world, consumer focus groups or retailers look at virtual mock-ups of new products on shelves. A pointer gives individuals a sense of moving through the aisle of a real store. Filippo Passerini, president, global business services and chief information officer, says:[8]

> *This technology allows us to implement quickly feedback on a product's packaging or artwork. Instead of taking five or six weeks to redesign a physical mock-up, we do it in days as it is all virtual reality. This allows us to iterate more times and still cut costs while bringing innovations to market much faster and better. Our virtual solutions are now used in almost 80% of all P&G's initiatives.*

Focusing on the profitable core

Over two-thirds of those surveyed highlighted how much they had focused on the profitable core of the business, and even more – four-fifths –predicted that this would be the case in future.

Ian Howells, general manager at Honda Europe, says:

> *When it comes to lessons about managing uncertainty, the first is that you will come out of the crisis at some point. But I've scribbled here "don't forget the knitting". You can't forget to pay attention to your core business. Stick to your knitting and make sure that you are concentrating on the day-to-day.*

Toyota has been counting the cost of losing its focus. As its chief executive, Akio Toyoda, said at an American congressional hearing:[9]

> *I would like to point out that Toyota's priority has traditionally been the following: first, safety; second quality; and third, volume. These priorities became confused, and we were not able to stop, think and make improvements as much as we were able to before, and our basic stance to listen to customers' voices to make better products has weakened somewhat.*

In contrast, Procter & Gamble has chosen to focus on its most profitable brands, customers and markets. Unilever has done the same, concentrating on its top 50 brands.

It can be difficult for firms to maintain operational focus when they are beset by prolonged turbulence and uncertainty. Chapter 3 emphasises the need for "navigational" leaders who can help their people get to grips with the uncertainties of the future.

Sull's advice is for companies to avoid being distracted by a proliferation of corporate priorities. Setting a cap at three or maybe up to five in any year will maintain focus and ensure scarce resources and management attention go to where they are most needed.

These priorities should be "must-win" battles. Brian Lowell, a partner at McKinsey, also suggests the usefulness of a "materiality test", such as whether 1% or 2% of a company's future earnings are at stake, to ensure companies are not overwhelmed with too many issues during times of "profound uncertainty".

However, too much focus can be as dangerous as too little, according to Eric Beinhocker of the McKinsey Global Institute:

Companies become so focused, they become honed machines for doing whatever it is that is succeeding today, at scale. They have a natural tendency to kill off variety. The problem is that whatever is succeeding today may not succeed in the future and a lot of the things that are succeeding in the future may not be succeeding today.

Firms can become entrenched in what Beinhocker calls "path dependencies". This is when focus becomes rigidity, with all of a firm's internal resources sucked into a set of activities. The result is that it becomes ever harder and more costly for the firm to step off the path. This can lead to a gradual narrowing of capability, especially in terms of operational flexibility and innovation, which is only noticed when there is a sudden, disruptive change in the environment and the organisation proves incapable of responding quickly.

Beinhocker advises that the best way to avoid this rigidity is to establish a portfolio of experiments:

You want your portfolio of experiments to be robust in the sense that it is covering enough of the landscape that if things change, you have some chance of being roughly in the right spot.

Now there is some confusion about this in that people are saying are you just randomly scattering stuff in the hope that a thousand flowers will bloom? No, you are using your best knowledge and analysis in how you construct this portfolio. You won't do lots of things for very good reasons and you won't get everything right

- you may even be the company that turns down the next Apple computer!

Now this is not diversity in the old sense of a diversified company. In your portfolio of experiments, you build on a platform of capabilities. The second solution is how you choose in this portfolio - where you double-down your bets and scale up, where you should be pulling back.

In uncertain environments, your selection process depends on getting the signals from the market, such as customer feedback, beamed back to the company as purely as possible. You have to try and keep those signals from being as undistorted as possible.

Beinhocker recommends a portfolio of initiatives. Business units should be encouraged to "fail small and succeed big" through small-scale experiments. A company can retain focus and also manage the cost implications of this approach by requiring its units not only to maintain these portfolios of initiatives but also to be cost competitive with their industry peers.

GlaxoSmithKline (GSK) is another company that is pursuing focused flexibility. The global pharmaceutical business is concentrating on building a strong portfolio in consumer health care, generic drugs, vaccines and biological medicines alongside its core franchise in patented chemical drugs. It has created a "Futures Group" to help concentrate marketing and research and development around an identified group of global brands.

GSK was concerned that a focus on global brands might cause a loss of innovative capability. The futures team wanted to encourage managers in national markets to keep coming up with new ideas about innovative products or how to take advantage of local market opportunities.

This led to the creation of the "Spark Network" within GSK's consumer health-care business. Marketing and R&D managers, or "sparkies", from around the world now hold regular teleconferences and web-enabled discussions and the occasional global meeting to share ideas.

"We used the word 'spark' because it was intended to light up GSK with new ideas and become a hotbed of creativity for the business," explains Peter Robbins, the former head of GSK's Spark Network, who now works at the Innovation Foundation at University College, Dublin.

The Spark Network is occasionally linked in to global meetings organised by the Future Group for the global brands to develop and incubate new ideas, platforms or territories by which to grow the brand.

However, when faced with fast-expiring drug patents and a need to accelerate the development of new drugs, GSK favours external alliances as a way of exploring a range of alternative or potentially contradictory trajectories in drug development.

Adrian Rawcliffe of GlaxoSmithKline explains:

> For us, it is the ability to hold dissonant thoughts within the same organisation that is key to being able to manage uncertainty. You've got to be able to place bets on things that have a low probability of success but a high upside and you've got to be able to do that in an organisation where you want a large majority of your people delivering a fairly stable "to plan" agenda.
>
> One of the ways we have chosen to do this for our drug development is an "externalisation" strategy, where we forge many different types of external alliances. It is easier to achieve if you can carve off that activity and you can say to yourself, "I know that our investment over here is based on a fundamentally different principle than our investment over there." Those two views are not consistent with each other. If I put them in the same organisation, there is going to be a fight to see which one wins but I don't want to do that, I want the best of both of them because they represent different views on the world.

Portfolio agility

A small number of those interviewed in the survey follow-up stressed the need to reshape their businesses through such means as acquisitions, joint ventures, alliances and outsourcing to respond to opportunities in their markets. For some companies, such reconfiguring is essential if you want to "reinvent" the business.

For some companies, the economic crisis had helped them recognise the importance of this kind of agility.

GlaxoSmithKline

We reinvent ourselves all the time. Three years ago, I dismantled one of our external alliances and integrated it back into the organisation, creating an internal centre of excellence. If you look at what is happening, our competitors are doing the same. If everything is on course and people are trying to imitate what you are doing, then you have to change. You have to reinvent yourself.

As your network of alliances grows bigger and bigger, for example, it can become unmanageable so you have to deconstruct. You change your strategy and you retrain your people. That is why flexible thinking is so important. We do something different but without losing the benefit of what we have learned. The question "what is likely to be different tomorrow than what we are doing today?" is very important. What is the creativity in people and how do you foster self-expression? The creativity then bubbles up.

Letizia Amadini-Lane

Kathleen Eisenhardt, a professor at Stanford University, has long advocated this type of agility. As far back as 2000, she and her colleague Shona Brown, then a McKinsey consultant, highlighted their research into the importance of regularly restructuring business portfolios as a response to "a world of shifting and dynamic markets".[10]

This capability is dubbed "patching". Their research revealed that "managers who patch make lots of small, frequent changes to their organisational structures". This enables them to align their organisation with opportunities for growth, disruptive change or markets that are evolving at different rates.

Patching includes splitting off parts of the business to focus on a specific market or customer segment, adding new product or service divisions, or spin-offs to exploit innovation. It involves reconfiguring different capabilities, such as combining a new business based on an

Balfour Beatty

The economic crisis really galvanised us as a business. I think it accelerated a lot of things that were in train anyway and gave them a real impetus. We're more aware of the need to be more revolutionary than evolutionary. We always knew we would need to expand into emerging markets, but since the crisis we are much more definite about how to do this. We have been much clearer about finding the right people and devising the right management structure, and how joint ventures and strategic alliances should be organised. It is all very deliberate and open – it is no longer a distant plan, it is under way.

Richard Gartside

emergent technology with a cash-rich business based on a mature but inevitably declining technology or market.

Eisenhardt and Brown argue that the ability to reshape a business is critical in turbulent markets. It is not the same as traditional restructuring; "while managers in stable markets associate structure with stability, managers in companies that patch believe structure is inherently temporary".

Donald Sull argues that this reconfiguring is so important that it should be classified separately as portfolio agility. He believes it is the most difficult form of agility:

I conducted a survey in 2010 of 450 senior executives with McKinsey & Co. We gave them ten questions to self-assess their organisation for the three different types of agility and by almost every measure of self-assessment, they struggled most with portfolio agility, so it's really tough.

McKinsey also did a separate study that compared top- and medium-performing firms for profitable growth over a 5-7 year period and concluded that two-thirds of the difference in performance is attributable to poor portfolio agility.[11]

Sull comments:

This is hugely important, especially if looking over longer periods of time. Look at Goldman Sachs, General Electric, even HSBC, where agility within individual units has been complemented with reallocating your portfolio and adapting at that level as well.

The downside of this type of agility is that business portfolios can become too complex and unwieldy, as Praful Pillay of SunGard India has experienced:

We have been engaged in a lot of acquisitions and we have been looking at rationalising some of our products. We have acquired so many products that we are in urgent need of a portfolio rationalisation exercise.

If this is done purely internally, you risk isolating yourself from the customer. It is really important for us to be alongside the customer, understanding the uncertainties that the customer is facing. We need to ensure we can align ourselves to our customers' business objectives as and when they change.

Sull has the final word:

It is shocking how many large companies with diversified portfolios do not have a process in place where they visualise their portfolios. They need some mechanism or framework to look at (whether it is the Boston Consulting Group cows and dogs – I have a preferred framework around stages in the life cycle of opportunities). It doesn't matter what you use, as long as you have some way of visualising your portfolio. Then, see where your portfolio is out of whack – do you have enough start-ups in the pipeline, are you trying to scale too many things or not enough, are your mature businesses about to fall over a cliff and go into decline? Have that discussion about what your portfolio looks like.

Organisational agility

Those interviewed in the survey follow-up spoke of the need to have flatter, more autonomous organisational structures that are capable of adapting to changes in the external environment. Such structures

GlaxoSmithKline

The higher the level of uncertainty, the more agile companies need to be. It is very difficult for companies with a single point of control to be agile – the entire organisation needs to move. Your organisation pivots on the person who is accountable for it. If there is one person at the top, then the entire organisation is the body doing the pivoting and it is only going to respond to very big things. What you actually want is everybody down the organisation forming clusters that pivot on each other so they can see external change and they are empowered to shift the organisation to respond.

If you go back several years to our R&D, we had about 12 people who made all the decisions, pretty much for an organisation of 70,000 (indeed some people would say it was one person, the chairman of R&D, who made all the decisions). We now have 100 people who are empowered to take decisions within their sphere. They do not need to go to anyone else.

Adrian Rawcliffe

empower employees at different levels to make decisions, share critical information, and forge close relationships with internal and external customers and suppliers.

For large global organisations like GSK, it is feasible to have a variety of organisational structures. This can be a way for a business to hedge its bets so that when the environment shifts, a company will have the ability to respond somewhere inside it.

An alternative strategy is to adapt a new organisational structure for the whole business. For instance, Gary Hamel, a management guru, has convincingly argued that the only way American businesses can compete against the "onslaught" of new competition from China and India is by moving to a more flexible, "networked and latticed style of organisation". He believes that traditional hierarchical structures are no longer fit for purpose for firms that need to constantly innovate in order to survive.

Traditional corporate structures are functional and hierarchical, tending to favour specialisation and product or service standardisation rather than flexibility and innovation. Hamel argues for flatter, more autonomous structures where work is based around self-managed teams. Creativity and innovation increase when the employees closest to the customer determine the what, how and when of work. The benefits include:

- improved engagement and satisfaction – employees are partners and collaborators, not just a "resource" to get things done;
- cross-functional capability – creating stronger and more adaptable individuals and teams;
- effective resource management – because the project team doing the work rather than a remote senior manager takes responsibility for self-scheduling;
- unlimited innovation – ideas can come from and be acted upon by anyone within the organisation;
- improved communication – information flows freely and transparently across the organisation;
- stronger relationships – with both internal and external customers.

In his book *The Future of Management* (co-authored with Bill Breen), Hamel highlights three innovative companies: Whole Foods Market, an American food retailer, W.L. Gore, an engineering company that invented Gore-Tex fabric, and Google, an internet and technology company.[12] These companies have attempted to move away from a hierarchical, "command and control" model. For example:

- Whole Foods has reorganised its structure around individual retail stores and empowered each team to manage its store autonomously, decide what stock to buy, hire and fire staff, and respond quickly to any changes in customer tastes or preferences. Performance data are shared with all employees and remuneration is based on team performance.
- W.L. Gore is highly innovative and has been granted more than 2,000 patents worldwide. The company has no formal hierarchy

and is organised around small, self-managed teams. Employees are allowed "dabble time" to come up with new ideas, which they can present to their managers at any time.

■ Google operates through small teams of talented people who are encouraged to pursue seemingly wild ideas. It advocates the "70–20–10 rule" – that is, the company should devote 70% of its engineering resources to its base business, 20% to services that might expand from that core and 10% to "fringe" ideas.

Other companies have tried to create such network-based organisations, but as the experiences of Cisco Systems and Netflix reveal, this is not a straightforward task.

Cisco Systems

Cisco Systems, the world's largest provider of internet networking and communications equipment, had to perform an embarrassing U-turn in May 2011 when it announced it was abandoning its much vaunted innovative management structure. Back in 2008, the company decided that its functional structure was too cumbersome and fragmented for an increasingly "intelligent, network-centric world", in the words of its chairman and chief executive, John Chambers.

Cisco introduced a flatter, more collaborative structure to enable it to manage cross-functional business priorities more effectively. Instead of a team of 5–10 executives, cross-functional, collaborative councils and boards would handle Cisco's "major priorities". The company tried to make these groups the equivalent of a social networking group by bringing together people with a range of relevant expertise who had the power to make and execute decisions rapidly.

Between 2008 and 2011, when Cisco believed it had a $10 billion opportunity in some new area of business, it created councils, a board for $1 billion opportunities and working groups for tactical projects that might be initiated by a council or board. A council was accountable to a board and a board was accountable to an operating committee, comprising 12 or so senior leaders. A board or council was authorised to start an initiative only when it could present a convincing strategy for becoming number one or two in a market segment. In the first year of the new leadership structure, Cisco went from managing an average of one or two cross-functional priorities to managing 22.

In 2008 Chambers made a confident assertion in *Harvard Business Review*:[13]

> We think this is what organisations of the future will look like and this 21st century leadership style will be a major competitive advantage for us over the next decade ... In this way, management can consider many, many opportunities spanning the capabilities of the company, instead of just viewing them by silo or function. This allows us to have constructive discussions, get buy-in and then execute rapidly.

The new structure caused considerable controversy, with some commentators being openly derisory about what they saw as an overly complicated structure that undermined rather than strengthened management accountability. The number of councils and boards appeared to have spiralled out of control; by 2009 there were 47 cross-functional boards and 12 councils.

Cisco's performance weakened, and in May 2011 the company announced it was restructuring once more. It consolidated its engineering and sales divisions and refocused its activities around five core areas driving the growth of networks and the internet. Cisco also announced it was reducing its councils from nine to three and its boards from 47 to 15.

Responding to an allegation on CNBC in December 2011 that the management structure was the cause of Cisco's "underperformance", Chambers denied this. He admitted, however:

> The board and council structure was too complex. We have moved from nine councils to three, focused on customers, moved the responsibility for decision-making to sales execs and engineering execs and moved from 42 boards to 15. What was a strength in one time of growth becomes a weakness in the other, and we have changed that ... the complexity of the business is a fair criticism.

Netflix

Netflix, the world's largest DVD rental and online video streaming business, has also had its fingers burned. Established in 1999, the company experienced rapid growth. Its stated goal is to be "big, fast and flexible". It has deliberately resisted putting in structures and rules that it believes might undermine staff's freedom to "make a big impact" or damage its "high-performance culture".

Well aware that a lack of processes might lead to chaos, Netflix chose instead to rely on a culture that tries to balance creativity with self-discipline and freedom with responsibility. The role of managers is to set the context for staff, not control their work. The company relies on networking among staff, regular departmental meetings, and openness and transparency in its strategies and business results.

Netflix appeared to do no wrong, and its informal, flexible structure appeared to give it an uncanny knack of anticipating the changing preferences of home-entertainment customers. However, Netflix made a disastrous decision in the second half of 2011. It decided to introduce a new pricing scheme. It also announced and then retracted a separate branding for DVDs. More than 800,000 subscribers cancelled their service, forcing the chief executive, Reed Hastings, to issue an apology for the company being "overconfident" and "moving too fast". "In hindsight, I slid into arrogance based on past success," he said at a press meeting outside the company's Californian headquarters.

In a letter to investors, Hastings said:[14]

> We compounded the problem with our lack of explanation about the rising cost of the expansion of streaming content, and steady DVD costs, so that absent of that explanation, many perceived us as greedy.

Netflix maintains that its pricing structure is sound and that insufficient communication was its primary error, but customers continue to send critical blog posts to the company accusing it of greed and arrogance.

Its informal and fast-moving structure has served the company well. However, the problems referred to above suggest that a high-performance culture that encourages big bold moves in the market can sometimes backfire if employees become overconfident and take their focus off the customer. Netflix's management philosophy accepts that it is operating in a "creative inventive market and not a safety critical market", and as such its deliberate choice to eschew rules and procedures that might inhibit its entrepreneurial culture will increase the risk of making mistakes. The company needs to rethink where it should place the boundary between control and freedom and how it defines what it calls "good" processes (that "help talented people get more done") and "bad" processes (that increase "complexity and rigidity").

Conclusion

To manage uncertainty well an organisation must be agile. Indeed, it needs four types of agility:

- **The financial agility** that depends principally on liquidity to give it a buffer against bad commercial weather and unexpected shocks, and that also gives it the freedom to pursue opportunities and experiment.

- **The operational agility** that comes from being lean and efficient.

- **The portfolio agility** to reshape, reinvent and reallocate resources with the speed that is at least desirable if not necessary.

- **The organisational agility** that usually comes with less hierarchical and more empowering structures.

Any firm that can achieve high levels of agility in these four categories will survive and thrive in uncertain times. But as any athlete knows you have to work at it – or you will soon get out of shape.

5 Resilience

The capability to absorb and build positively on adversity, shocks and setbacks

Resilience is the ability to take a knock, dust yourself down and start again.

Richard Gartside, Balfour Beatty

If leaders can only be negative about the future, a sense of helplessness and paralysis sinks in. The business begins to feel it is a victim and that it cannot do anything positive to shape its future.

Learning and development manager, defence technology manufacturer

ORGANISATIONS MUST BE RESILIENT if they are to survive in uncertain and volatile times. If they are, they will be better able to adjust to sudden disruptive change and cope with sustained stress and pressure.

Resilience goes hand in hand with agility. As companies seize the advantage or neutralise a threat (open a new factory or close a poorly performing business unit), they must be resilient enough to handle the disruption and uncertainty their actions have triggered.

A resilient organisation is more likely to face up to unexpected change and remain focused on performance. Less resilient organisations are more likely to ignore or underplay the potential effects of external shocks, or may simply be overwhelmed by them. Organisations that lack resilience are all too likely to become locked in a downward spiral of performance.

By definition, a crisis has a definite beginning and end. Some form of resolution is reached, whether positive – survival and/or recovery – or negative, such as the business being split up and sold off, or total closure. In a crisis, companies typically switch to crisis management and embark on a high-speed programme of change. Managers swing into action and channel their energy and skill into dealing with the crisis. Because of their experiences in the various recessions and downturns of the past two decades, many companies are good at crisis management.

Periods of prolonged uncertainty lack the immediate intensity of a crisis and therefore require a different – deeper and more embedded – kind of resilience. Uncertainty saps morale and energy more. Managers and their staff cannot anticipate how long the uncertainty will last, when they will need to act and how the various sources of uncertainty will affect their part of the business. This creates space for doubt and anxiety to set in. As tried and tested assumptions no longer work, managers who are not resilient may lose confidence and become defensive and inflexible.

The managing uncertainty survey and follow-up interviews carried out for this book, together with previous research, reveal that resilience has several traits. It involves:

- adapting to stressful circumstances and not being overwhelmed or paralysed;
- bouncing back from shocks or setbacks and not being locked in denial or anger;
- focusing on performance and high-priority goals and avoiding becoming introspective and distracted;
- staying positive and energetic;
- staying "humble" and open to new thinking and not being arrogant or defensive;
- focusing on solutions and opportunities and not exaggerating or becoming obsessive about problems and potential threats;
- learning from experience and not becoming fearful about the future.

From denial and paralysis ...

Very senior people in our company deny the need to think or talk about uncertainty. People are afraid of engaging in any discussion around uncertainty, they are afraid to speak openly about the uncertainties of our future. We have a very conservative and status oriented culture and this stops difficult or challenging (to the status quo) conversation across the organisation.

This manager, working for a leading defence technology manufacturer, believes the future looks bleak for her firm. She believes that her company is poorly positioned to deal with the turbulence in international markets as some of its largest governmental customers make severe spending cuts. Although her firm cannot realistically shape these events, she believes it can still take some positive steps to prepare for the new reality:

If you deny the present, you are in deep trouble. Managing uncertainty requires a new way of thinking. You can't change what you can't change. But leaders can and must focus on where they can make a difference.

... to acceptance and practical solutions

I think that our own perceptions of the last two years have changed in terms of the way we handle the ambiguity that is there. I think we have grown up in the last two years – in our willingness and our ability to cope with diverging bits of information and opinion ... I have certainly seen with us a willingness to accept that strategy A was wrong and that we must rethink and reshape.

Focusing on solutions has led to Ceridian taking a much more flexible approach to strategic planning (explored in Chapter 2). It has also helped the company understand its customers better, many of whom are experiencing uncertainty themselves and consequently delaying their investment decisions.

Nick Laird, Ceridian's chief commercial officer, comments:

If they are not sure where the revenues are going, and they are not sure what level of investment they should be making into their own plans, we tend to find that the "sit on one's hands and do nothing" scenario is the preferred response.

However, drawing upon its own experience of managing uncertainty, Ceridian is now focusing on developing new services that will be particularly valuable to clients struggling with uncertainty.

As Laird concludes:

We are putting a lot of effort into externalising something that is currently intrinsic – it's about turning our knowledge into an asset which can provide something of a punch to a new customer. For example, we spent a lot of time teasing out our waste-reducing skills. What does that mean? How does it work? What are the benefits of it? Why is that different from the next supplier? So you are therefore able to articulate your offer in an unusual and effective way.

Avoiding taking responsibility

Speed is often needed if the business just has to stay on its feet – for example, you may need to cut costs fast. If events are moving rapidly and managers are too slow to decide on a course of action, these decisions will be taken out of their hands and the events will dictate how they react. Sometimes, managers half-consciously allow this to happen, and it is often because they are working in a blame culture where no one wants to be accountable. They almost want the hard decisions to be taken for them.

Chris Stephenson
States of Jersey

Learning from past experience

I am old enough to remember various shocks and upheavals such as the oil crisis of the 1970s and the three-day working week in the UK. A lot of my learning has come from reflecting on my experience of various recessions in the past two decades. If companies and individuals cannot learn from the past, they will not be able to shape the future.

I think my organisation could have looked more deliberately at how other similar economic trends were playing out, in other parts of the world or in the past. We could have looked at what lessons we could learn. For example, we could have looked at how Japanese companies responded to a stagnating Japanese economy – how did they manage in those circumstances?

Manager working for a UK National Health Service programme during the financial crisis

The interviewees revealed that living in uncertain times is a psychologically tough and often exhausting experience. Executives spoke about the shocks and disruptions as their businesses were hit by the financial crisis and economic turbulence. As they looked ahead to the next 3–5 years, they saw only continuing uncertainty.

The following examples provide a snapshot of the challenges of remaining resilient in the face of a highly unpredictable and complex business environment.

Developing more resilient managers and businesses

What makes some managers more resilient than others? Why do some rise to the challenge and work harder and better, while less hardy managers struggle and even break down under the strain? What makes some companies more resilient than others, appearing to relish the challenge of uncertainty, while others struggle to accept that the old certainties have disappeared for the moment at least and perhaps permanently?

Positive, forward thinking

That's where optimism comes in, it's not blind optimism, it's about taking a more optimistic view of the future, having confidence in the brand, confidence in the work we do. Then you're ready to think about positioning yourself for the growth that will come out the other end, but it is hard because people can get stuck in a negative mindset.

Curling up in a foetal ball is the worst thing you can do. You have to take control. It's uncomfortable, it's painful, but it's much better to engage and start to make decisions. You might not like where it takes you, but you will be in control and that will be much better.

Dan Flint
Simmons & Simmons

Taking control

Staff empowerment is encouraged in my organisation. We have an expression called "spirited independence" which is really to encourage our associates to "do the right thing" and giving them the authority to do that. There are limits to this but our culture says that if you see an opportunity, you should present it to your senior manager or a senior member of the Board and say, "I think this is an idea that is going to run".

This is fine in normal circumstances but when you get into an environment of high uncertainty, people don't know quite where to turn. Therefore the whole thing starts to freeze up a bit. You don't quite get the drive. I was coming in from the outside at about that time and part of my DNA was to stop people just looking at the paperwork on the desk and dealing with that. You are almost too frightened to look ahead to see what is coming.

Ian Howells
Honda Europe

The survey follow-up interviews reveal that the pressures and disruptions affecting businesses vary hugely and that the resilience demonstrated by a business is also influenced by its agility. Some companies have moved wisely and speedily and in doing so have alleviated the destructive pressures on the business. It must also be true that it is easier to be resilient when you believe your company is making winning moves. Less resilient and less agile companies have either made the wrong moves or not moved at all. In this context, staff can be dragged down by well-founded anxieties and frustration about their uncertain future.

Joshua Margolis, an associate professor at Harvard Business School, and Paul Stoltz, chief executive of Peak Learning, a research and consultancy firm, say:[1]

> Contemporary adversity is like a two-headed hydra ... Firstly, managers are confronting in rapid succession challenges the likes of which they have never seen before: a worldwide economic crisis, the globalisation of business, the rise of new technologies, deep demographic shifts. Feeling discouraged and helpless, they turn away from the problems. Secondly, if these managers went to their bosses for guidance, they would most likely receive inadequate coaching. That is because most supervisors, riding their own waves of hard-won successes, lack the empathy to intervene effectively.
>
> Whatever their reaction, the challenge for today's manager is to turn a negative experience into a productive one – that is, to counter adversity with resilience.

Personal resilience is influenced by such factors as personality, cultural background, motivation, beliefs and values, but also by professional training and organisational culture and the behaviours it instils. Researchers have studied the qualities and behaviours of resilient people today in order to determine how much resilient managers are born that way and how much their resilience is made. Below is what they have found.

Less of "we're right" and more humility

Our organisation is highly intelligent. The lowest grade in the R&D operation is a PhD. We are scientists and we can be a little too much in love with our own opinions. Admitting that there may be better solutions outside the company is not easy for us. So flexible thinking and a little humility were required to make our ongoing strategy of external collaboration work – and it is something that we need to keep looking at.

My method is to engage the people effectively. You don't change an organisation. You change people. You need to take it one person at a time. You don't change attitude and culture by computers or through a course. You have to be on the floor, you have to challenge people, you have to work with them and you have to put a lot of energy into the process. It is a very tiring job but it is what you do.

Letizia Amadini-Lane
GlaxoSmithKline

We aim to build up over time a leadership which is "strategically humble" in the sense of understanding that there are many things that are influencing them and that in order to address these, leaders need to look through the eyes of others. This helps them to see how those patterns of behaviour and choice may be different from what they would assume and recognise that there is a breadth of outcome over which they do not have control.

Jeremy Bentham
Vice-president, global business environment
Royal Dutch Shell

The roots and traits of resilience

Studies by psychologists into why some individuals demonstrate "hardiness" and "mental toughness" have concluded that in essence it comes down to be a blend of personality and attitude.

Two recently developed frameworks, for example, define resilience as a composite of attitudes, motivations and behaviours. The first was developed during 2008–09 and used with South African companies by Rod Warner, head of the Building Resilience Group (BRG), a consultancy based in South Africa. BRG undertook an analysis of how people deal with adversity at work,[2] which helped shape its findings that resilience in an organisational setting produces resilient employees who:

- are better able to resist stressful experiences;
- remain focused;
- deal with multiple demands;
- stay calm and healthy;
- emerge from the adversity stronger and more resourceful.

BRG's framework is based on seven principles, which are summarised in Table 5.1.

The second framework has been developed by Ashridge business school and is also based on seven attributes demonstrated by resilient managers (see Table 5.2).[3] Perhaps not surprisingly, the two frameworks share a lot in common.

Developing resilience in managers

The two frameworks featured above suggest that personal resilience is just that – highly personal. Two individuals facing the same challenge may react very differently. What can organisations do to help their employees become more resilient?

One way is to help people become more aware of the thinking processes that can make them more or less resilient. These processes are semi-conscious but they programme people's responses to difficult situations. If thinking is largely negative, each difficult experience reinforces this negatively, and the converse is also true. With help and support, individuals can uncover these hidden assumptions, habitual thoughts and ingrained beliefs. They can then alter how they think and respond to challenges, setbacks or failures.

Stoltz and Margolis believe that uncovering ingrained reactions to

TABLE 5.1 **BRG's seven principles of resilience**

A strong sense of purpose and meaning	"In times of adversity this becomes very important as it directly addresses the issue of why persevere rather than just giving up"
Self-knowledge	Managers have a realistic insight into their own character, strengths and "vulnerabilities". This is the basis for understanding their capabilities and limits when dealing with adversity
Maintaining perspective	Resilient individuals find positive ways to distract themselves from the stress of adversity. This enables them to "recharge their batteries" and return to the challenge with renewed energy
Positive feeling	This involves reining in negative thinking and actively generating positive thoughts about a situation
Realistic optimism	Choosing to look at the best possible outcome of a situation but basing this optimism in reality – otherwise disappointment will inevitably follow
Perseverance	Mainly through being open minded and flexible. However, too little results in surrender and defeat but too much can result in a "blinkered and bull-headed approach". Other symptoms include tunnel vision, minimal listening and applying brute force to the difficult situation
Reaching out to others	Both to offer help and to ask for help

Source: Warner, 2009

adversity is one of the most powerful means of helping individuals to become more resilient.

Managers often make quick assumptions about the causes of the adversity as well as its magnitude, likely impact and how long the difficulty will last. When facing chaotic or unforeseen events, managers can of course make very wrong assumptions. If they are to become more resilient, they need to untangle these assumptions.

As well as faulty thinking, Stoltz and Margolis believe that most people fall into two emotional traps when dealing with difficult situations. One that especially afflicts successful managers is "deflation" or a sense of disappointment and angst when adversity strikes. Unable to fix a problem, these managers can be swamped by such feelings, directed inwards and towards others, and feel mistreated, dispirited and even besieged. The other trap is

TABLE 5.2 **Ashridge's personal resilience framework**

Purpose	The extent to which an individual has structure, commitment and meaning present in their life
Challenge	The way in which an individual perceives situations, solves problems and manages change
Emotional control	The way in which individuals control their emotions in situations and how they attribute this control
Balance	How individuals choose to view the world and the distribution of care and attention given to aspects in their life
Determination	An individual's ability to remain motivated and to carry on after difficulty or adversity
Self-awareness	Belief in themselves and their capabilities, as well as the accuracy of these self-estimations
Awareness of others	Individuals' awareness of others and how this affects how they behave, including how individuals communicate, interact and empathise with others

Source: Ashridge, 2011

victimisation. Managers assume the role of an innocent bystander, which requires strenuous efforts to justify events and ward off both criticism and helpful advice.

One way out of this blind alley is for managers to adopt a way of thinking that enables them to focus on what they can do to improve the situation. Stoltz and Margolis call this response-oriented thinking. They have identified "four lenses through which managers can view adverse events to make this shift effectively" (see Table 5.3).

Managers can apply a set of questions to each lens to move them away from negative and towards responsive thinking. They should practise this "resilience regime" to ensure it becomes second nature, not something reserved for a crisis. For example:

- Specifying questions help managers identify ways to intervene, such as "what aspects of the situation can I directly influence to change the course of this adverse event?".

- Visualising questions help shift managers' attention away from the difficult event or situation towards a more positive outcome,

TABLE 5.3 **Response-oriented thinking: four lenses**

Lens 1 Control over the situation	Rather than becoming victims or feeling powerless, managers should think positively about how to take control of the situation. The goal is to generate possibilities rather than a detailed plan of action
Lens 2 The impact of the situation	It is important not to focus on negatives or feel angry or victimised. Managers need to consider how they can influence the outcome of events. How can they make the most immediate positive impact?
Lens 3 The breadth of adversity	It is futile to worry about how far the black cloud of adversity will extend. The real question is how to limit the damage and look for opportunities in the midst of chaos
Lens 4 The duration of adversity	No one has a crystal ball to tell them how long adversity will last. There will always be some who think it will "blow over soon" and others who see it continuing for years (as many do of the post-financial crisis downturn). Stoltz and Margolis's advice is to think about the desired outcome for the business and identify some positive steps that can be taken to move in that direction

Source: Stoltz and Margolis, 2010

such as "what would the manager I most admire do in this situation?".

■ "Collaborating" questions encourage managers to consider joint problem-solving and action, such as "which member of my team can help me and what is the best way of engaging him or her?".

Stoltz has developed a diagnostic tool known as the Adversity Quotient (AQ) Profile, which guides users through 14 scenarios, each followed by the four types of questions, to gauge resilience.

BRG has also pioneered a measurement tool to help individuals "build" resilience known as the Personal Resilience Questionnaire.[4] This is a 35-item questionnaire based on BRG's seven traits of resilience which has been used since 2009 with South African organisations such as Old Mutual, City of Cape Town, and a number of local, provincial and national government departments. BRG has identified various practical steps to help build each aspect of resilience and holds workshops on the topic.

Rod Warner concludes:

Is resilience teachable? The answer is a resounding yes. Our research has revealed that the innate skills relating to building resilience can be developed and enhanced through training.

For example, negative thinking and "persistent negative self-talk" can be reframed. Individuals can be helped to find alternative ways to think about a problem.

Other ways of reframing are to choose milder and less calamitous ways of expressing the adversity or to change statements into questions, and then to focus on finding the answers to these.

Ashridge piloted its 53-item questionnaire with a sample of 136 participants working in UK-based organisations at the end of 2011[5] and is now using it with a large UK charity. The questionnaire is used as a development tool to help managers become aware of their own level of resilience and where they might be "depleted" or especially "well resourced". Managers are encouraged to think about what they have learned from continual or acute pressure. They then look forward by considering what might test them in the future and how they can take steps to ensure they are ready to meet these challenges with resilience.

The message is that individuals can become more resilient by recognising how they think about and respond in difficult circumstances. Individuals can reshape their responses to ensure they develop the capacity to respond quickly and constructively to future uncertainty or crisis.

Helping managers to become more resilient is not about wrapping them in cotton wool or involving them in classroom discussion. Resilience comes through the crucible of experience. The more resilient managers become, the better they are at turning negative experiences into positive ones, and the stronger they become, and so it goes on.

As Warner concludes:

While no one chooses to experience tough times, successfully dealing with adversity does have an upside. Personal growth and development occur most when one is in unfamiliar territory, when comfort levels are breached and when one is out of one's depth and

Lloyds TSB

The City of London was shocked by the sudden stepping down of Lloyds TSB's newly appointed chief executive, António Horta-Osório, in November 2011. On the morning it was due to appear in front of a joint House of Commons and House of Lords committee alongside the chief executives of the UK's three other major bank, Lloyds made the announcement that Horta-Osório was suffering from "chronic fatigue" and would be taking an extended leave of absence.

Horta-Osório had taken up his appointment only eight months before, to a fanfare of praise from investors, politicians and fellow bankers. He was widely seen as the right man for the job of making the hard decisions required for Lloyds' restructuring and recovery plan. Indeed, the *Financial Times* predicted in May 2011 that Horta-Osório would be "the most ruthless" of the UK's bank bosses.[8]

Horta-Osório reportedly followed a gruelling work schedule but the scale of challenges facing Lloyds took their toll and he was forced to step aside for six weeks. According to *The Times*, the chief executive proposed on his return to work a plan to restructure and reduce his direct report lines to ensure he did not fall prey to exhaustion again. The newspaper alluded to rumours that the real situation was that shareholders had successfully insisted that Horta-Osório's responsibilities should be "diluted".[9]

struggling. Adversity creates such an environment, and a response based on resilience enables growth and development and even life-enhancing change to take place.

Stoltz and Margolis have a similar message:

Paradoxically, building resilience is best done precisely when times are most difficult – when we face the most upending challenges, when we are at the greatest risk of misfiring with our reactions,

GlaxoSmithKline

Complexity is not a bad thing. We have been involved in a journey where we have concluded that there are some areas where it is to our advantage to maintain complexity.

We have, for example, a geographic focus at the moment. That involves a huge amount of complexity. But the fact that we have a general manager in each country who has a relationship with the government and runs that business is a huge source of advantage to us. It gives us real-time ability to make decisions and develop strategy (through boots on the ground). It's great because that adds value.

What doesn't add value is 128 different financial reporting systems. So in those areas that add value, we are happy to maintain complexity – but we are going to be ruthless in stripping out the wrong form of complexity.

Adrian Rawcliffe

when we are blindest to the opportunities presented. At times like these, managers can counter adversity with resilience.

Complexity: a barrier to resilience?

Companies that are trying to be more agile face the danger of creating increasingly complex internal systems and structures. As international companies restructure, regroup their assets, speed up processes and strip away non-core activities through outsourcing and offshoring, they create new linkages and interdependencies. Corporate life becomes labyrinthine, with a proliferating number of processes to try to manage this internal complexity. Staff can become overloaded and the business as a whole can grind to a halt.

Theorists have explored how companies adapt to the complexity of their environments and in the process become overly complex themselves. Eric Beinhocker of the McKinsey Global Institute calls this problem a "complexity catastrophe":

Companies can become maladaptive. This happens in biological
systems as well. Let's say that companies are reflecting the pressures
of the environment but it may not be in a good way. There is a
phenomenon that shows up in biological systems and in computer
systems and in other complex systems.
As things get more complex, the number of nodes in the network
increase, and the number of interactions between the nodes increase.
You eventually get a kind of gridlock – what is called a complexity
catastrophe. You see it in organisations, you see it in eco-systems,
and you get this kind of collapse.
One issue certainly in terms of the financial crisis was the
complexity of the system. It got ahead of regulators and the
participants themselves. I was at an interesting meeting with a group
of banking chief executives and one of the participants said 'okay,
honestly guys, how many of you understood all the products and
services you were supplying and the risks associated with them
– raise your hands' – and nobody raised their hands. And that's
because what had been created surpassed the human capacity to
understand it all.

At some point there must be a trade-off between agility and
resilience. GlaxoSmithKline has thought this through and reached
the conclusion that complexity should be managed. The right type
of complexity can add value to the business; the wrong kind of
complexity, which damages resilience and agility, should be stripped
out.

Rawcliffe's comments reflect the findings of a study of complexity
by McKinsey in 2007 looking at how organisations can "crack the
complexity code" (building on Beinhocker's original research).[6] The
research looked at institutional complexity, the nodes and interactions
within an organisation which can proliferate as a business operates
in more countries, serves more customers, and offers more products
and services. It also looked at how individual employees experience
and deal with complexity – "in plain English, how hard it is to get
things done".

The study reveals that complexity can be managed in such a
way that companies stay both agile and resilient. The research team,

headed by Suzanne Heywood, a partner at McKinsey, discovered the following:

- Greater institutional complexity does not necessarily make life more difficult for individual employees.

- Institutional complexity can be exploited to pursue more value creating strategies.

- Organisations with lower levels of "individual complexity" (ie, that individual employees experienced as less complex) had the highest returns on capital employed and returns on invested capital.

- Companies that manage complexity are arguably harder to imitate.

The study concludes that institutional complexity underpins agility and that agile companies can manage increased institutional complexity if they reduce the resilience-damaging complexity experienced by individuals. This can be achieved through the following three steps:

- **Improve organisational design to minimise complexity.** The study suggests that centralised or decentralised decision-making does not matter, as long as companies eliminate duplication and make accountability and targets clear at the individual level.

- **Eliminate misaligned processes.** Companies with well-integrated systems and processes (for instance co-ordination between strategy and human resources) created less complexity for individuals.

- **Build managerial capabilities.** These include general management skills and the ability to take the initiative and work beyond a formally defined role or responsibility. The more managers can do this, the less complexity is a problem in an organisation.

McKinsey develops these ideas even further by providing a diagnostic approach helping managers spot "complexity hotspots" in their organisations.[7]

Developing a more resilient organisation

How can firms build collective resilience when they cannot predict what will be the next challenge or crisis to hit them? Based on the managing uncertainty survey follow-up interviews and other evidence, here are some of the steps that can help.

Shore up your decision-making processes

Interviewees spoke repeatedly of the dangers of being paralysed and overwhelmed by the scale of uncertainty facing them. It is essential for leaders to focus on the areas where they can take action and to clarify where it is a case of "watchful waiting". This can ensure employees do not become unnecessarily anxious but remain positive and focused.

Build trust between leaders and teams

Employees need to have confidence in their leaders, even when there is an unclear strategy or vision for the future (see Chapter 3).

Use people to change people

This is a maxim beloved by change-management experts, but it is arguably even more effective during times of uncertainty. In the face of uncertainty and unclear or contradictory evidence, people naturally turn to others, especially those they respect, to gain their insights. What they say (realism) and how they say it (optimism and confidence) can speak volumes compared with an internal announcement.

GlaxoSmithKline particularly values how such people can break down complacency and keep the organisation on its toes. Adrian Rawcliffe says:

> Seed the right type of people at critical parts of the organisation. There are people who are change agents and who are constantly restless and not satisfied. And there are people who are not. Positioning those people who are where you need change and having enough of them is the key to combating complacency.

GlaxoSmithKline

Crisis management gets a bad reputation. But actually GSK is at its best when it is managing a crisis. We had the case of the flu pandemic where suddenly we went from a situation where literally nobody wanted our flu products to Barack Obama saying, "How many doses can I get for my population?" Presidents of countries were calling up our local general manager, saying that "you need to supply this fast" – and we had a shortage of supply.

Understanding that circumstance, we opened up manufacturing lines overnight, we put whole vaccine strains on hold, we committed half the manufacturing organisation of vaccines to shipping the stuff, we went through a needs-based analysis so that we had a scientific approach to how we would supply that wasn't just based on who could pay the most.

We supplied countries as and when it looked like they were going to be hit by the pandemic. It was a whole response driven by about five other people on a daily basis. It was classic crisis management stuff. When you have that singular purpose, all other issues disappear other than achieving the goal in mind – and it is fantastic.

Well I agree that some aspects of [this performance] are unsustainable. It is difficult to operate an organisation of 100,000 people at that flat-out pace. However, there are aspects of that that I feel are very useful and that in little ways we should be emulating. I would argue that managing more of our organisation more of the time with some of the parameters of crisis management would be useful – particularly around the transparency and efficiency of decision-making during periods of crisis.

Adrian Rawcliffe

Make sure employees engage with the strategy

Work hard to ensure employees engage with the strategy of the business, even when this can be more accurately described as emergent than fully formed. Keep employees in the picture about the strategy and priorities so that they have enough information to use their own discretion in order to do their job most effectively. This also ensures that they play their part in executing any sudden changes in direction that the business might make to create an advantage or defend its position.

Avoid being overprotective

Be open with employees about the uncertainty facing the business and do not shield them from bad news or the actions of aggressive competitors. A false sense of security can turn into anger and betrayal if adversity strikes. More aware employees will become distrustful or overanxious, and in the absence of solid information will rely on rumour and guesswork.

Provide employees with opportunities to become more resilient

Experience is the best teacher. Key staff and those with high potential should be given opportunities, preferably before a crisis hits, to work in pressured, fast-moving parts of the business, with support built in to ensure they are not tested beyond their limits. They could be transferred to a smaller operating unit that is more entrepreneurial and nimble or a business that is struggling to obtain a foothold in an emerging market. Companies with external suppliers or alliance partners could consider transfers into these very different operating contexts.

Build a resilient culture

Allow people to express their concerns and admit to setbacks and challenges. Honest dialogue between leaders and followers is a constant theme in the survey follow-up interviews. Leaders must be frank about their own struggles if they want their teams to flag up dilemmas and problems caused by uncertainty. Openness encourages

---

Honda Europe

Your talent tends to raise the top during periods of uncertainty. They will develop that capability of looking up and looking out. Don't lose those moments because sometimes they can be a little fleeting.

You'll see that approach quite quickly and particularly in senior management where you might not see these people regularly – you might miss something by your normal talent management process.

It's a matter of working out who are the guys who are going to respond to the challenge and see you through this. Are they the same people that we identified before in calmer times? So I'd be really increasing the speed of my talent review, rather than doing a regular once a year check.

Ian Howells

---

a positive attitude and discourages a focus on blame. This makes it easier for staff to admit to setbacks and focus on the desired goals.

View crises or setbacks as valuable learning opportunities

You can learn a lot from the past, especially in terms of overcoming weaknesses.

Make resilience a core consideration

When taking any major decision make resilience a core consideration and build it into your organisation development strategy. Review how any major change is implemented to ensure that people are not being unnecessarily overloaded by stressful disruption.

Speaking about the need to keep people focused on the external environment, GlaxoSmithKline's Letizia Amadini-Lane stresses the importance of "listening":

It is an organisational development role. For us it is very important to keep playing this role and being present, listening to the organisation. We are changing all the time and the environment in which we operate is changing all the time. So we need to evaluate constantly what that means for our people. It is not enough to change the structure. You have to change the people.

Build in space for staff to talk about uncertainty

This is especially important in any change management programmes. Such initiatives can paradoxically generate more uncertainty and anxiety, as happened in a global media company that was undergoing a major restructuring programme. Senior managers were working flat out to implement the changes, building new teams and often moving location. A number of them were exhausted and anxious about the uncertainty around traditional versus e-books. However, charged with communicating a new direction and vision for the business, some felt that raising questions or concerns would be akin to an act of treachery.

Review management development processes

Ensure that management development and talent management processes nurture managers who are resilient and initiate debate about what it means to be personally resilient and resilient as an organisation. If some sort of definition of resilience is adopted, incorporate it consistently across the organisation in training, coaching and other personal development activities.

Stoltz says coaching skills in resilience are sorely needed:

Even the most resilient managers run into trouble trying to coach direct reports in crisis. They react with either a "how to" pep talk delivered utterly without empathy or understanding, or a sympathetic ear and reassurance that things will turn out okay. Neither response will equip their team to handle the next unforeseen twist or turn.

The survey follow-up interviews suggest that managers can also find the task of leading through uncertainty an exhausting and

Ford Motor Company

Neil Schloss believes a strong sense of identity and loyalty helped bring the company through some of its darkest days. Asked whether the company's resilience had been fatally sapped by all its troubles both before and during the financial crisis, he replied:

> We had a lot of energy in 2008–2009, it was not a case of being exhausted or paralysed. We were motivated by a mixture of desire and fear of not succeeding. There was no way the executive team would let the business go – we were united by the will to survive.
>
> Most of us had been in the company for years, we were home-grown Ford managers, we had worked there for 20 or 30 years. So yes, we had loyalty to the company, we have a sense of family. We also have a sense of pride and excitement working for a company that is so instrumental in the global economy and where the complexity and challenge of our business is so much greater compared with many businesses.

difficult experience. A number of interviewees spoke of conflict and division among the senior management team. Coaching may be helpful in such circumstances, as it can help a management team explore the nature of the challenges facing them and also provide discreet support to individuals who are struggling to adjust.

Provide stability through a sense of shared identity

When a business is in flux, a strong sense of identity can provide staff with stability and purpose. A collective sense of corporate identity is a powerful means of motivating staff and connecting with customers. In times of uncertainty, this organisational glue is even more vital.

The importance of identity was cited by a number of interviewees, with identity being variously described as the company "DNA", the "true north of the business", "our creative core" and "our raison d'être".

A 2009 report, *Strategy Evolution: Adapting to a New World*, by

Stanton Marris, a UK-based strategy consultancy, also highlights the importance of organisational identity. Based on interviews with 45 senior executives in 2009, it looked at the internal, hidden risks to strategy "when the external threat is substantial and unpredictable". The report describes organisational identity (or the "distinctive personality" of a firm) as "something of a secret weapon" in strategy development and execution for firms operating in certain environments. And it concludes:

When leaders uncover their organisational identity – comprising history, culture, beliefs and real (rather than official) values – and articulate it clearly, it becomes a tool to inform and guide the strategy process.

The benefits of a strong organisational identity are:

- it makes strategy real for people by linking into who they are collectively;
- it makes people more personally passionate about making it work by reflecting their own activity, for example in the strategic plan;
- it creates a point of stability when everything else is changing, for example by positioning the strategy in the organisation's history, so that it is seen as evolution rather than a break;
- it helps strategy become a more iterative and responsive process, for example by drawing in ideas from those in the middle of the business, especially those who hold important "collective memories" from the organisation's past.

Conclusion

Organisational resilience is especially important in the context of uncertain environments. The survey follow-up interviews with senior executives suggest that resilience should be seen as a capability in its own right. This capability ensures that individuals and an organisation collectively remain positive and focused during prolonged uncertainty. When the time comes to act effectively, there is enough energy and commitment for successful execution. Resilience and agility are therefore tightly interlinked capabilities.

Random House

At Random House the executive team was concerned to act in a way that helped staff to adapt and remain resilient to the uncertainties of the publishing industry. Neil Morrison recalls:

> It was a very difficult time. I had just joined the business. We were also looking at a gloomy economic and consumer spending outlook. Like many organisations, we felt we needed to look at our cost base. Inevitably much of this cost comes down to people.
>
> In terms of keeping the business resilient, a key decision was that if we were going to cut jobs, we would cut deep and once only. If we were going to lose people, we needed to make the tough decisions, but make them all together, rather than making reductions, then further reductions. It leaves everyone in a hugely uncertain, hermetically sealed environment.
>
> People are walking around wondering, "Am I going to be here next week?" In our industry we want people to be thinking creatively and being innovative and entrepreneurial. If they are feeling so uncertain, they are probably not doing much of that.
>
> After the job losses we also invested in the organisation in terms of encouraging creativity and innovation to help people understand that we were through that period of time. But it has to be said, people still struggle with some of those decisions.
>
> In terms of investing in creativity, we got in a number of different speakers to talk about creativity in their industries and what they were doing. Our aim was to give people headspace and to say "we are not going to focus on doing something, it is to give you time to think, reflect, talk to other people, share creative ideas, talk about our customers, what they want, and how that is changing".
>
> Our focus was to provide information and certainty to people to help them move forward. It was the right thing to do and in a creative industry it was easier to do, because everyone understands that to create and innovate, you need to pull away from the day-to-day business and have some headspace.

6   Open collaboration

The capability to dissolve boundaries, forge links and reach outside through partnerships and the sharing of ideas and information to gain a broader perspective and maximise innovation

> One positive step towards learning to live with uncertainty is to break down the walls of the organisation and connect with the external world. Managers in the organisation need to learn to hear, listen and collaborate with a diverse range of people. This needs to extend to the ability to develop trusting collaborative relationships with other companies.
>
> However, these relationships cannot be built slowly over time in the way that used to be possible. The future is changing very fast and if companies are to keep pace with these shifting possibilities, they need to give and take trust very quickly in their collaborative partnerships.
>
> Learning and development manager, defence technology manufacturer

FIRMS ARE OPERATING in an increasingly complex and interconnected world. The forces of globalisation and technology are sweeping away boundaries in markets and commercial sectors, making it ever harder for firms to map their external environment and strategic context. Faced with this complexity, no firm can afford to go it alone.

Through collaboration, a firm can reach beyond its boundaries, both mental and organisational, and link with others to understand and anticipate sources of uncertainty and their potential impact.

Collaboration becomes a powerful means of adapting to

FIG 6.1 **Sources used most to explore the impact of a crisis**

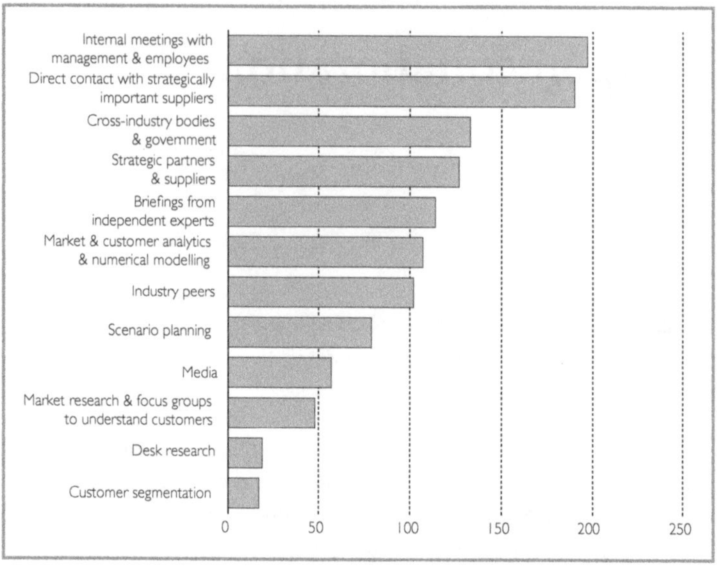

Source: © PA Knowledge 2011

an uncertain environment. Through linking up with external organisations and customers, a firm can try to resolve confusion, uncertainty and mixed signals from the environment.

Collaboration can help a firm absorb new ideas and perspectives from a diverse array of collaborative partners. This enhances a firm's ability to spot sudden shifts in customer or competitive behaviour, or the emergence of disruptive technology. Ultimately, the ability to collaborate will help a firm to keep learning and innovating.

The managing uncertainty survey carried out for this book and the follow-up interviews suggest that the financial crisis and continuing volatility emphasised the importance of firms staying close to stakeholders, such as employees, strategically important customers, cross-industry bodies and government organisations, and strategic partners and suppliers (see Figure 6.1).

The survey responses suggest that firms placed a priority on direct contact with their principal stakeholders instead of relying on

Random House

When a major UK book distributor went out of business, we urgently needed to find a route to the supermarkets. Other publishers had the same problem. A critical relationship was the Publishers Association where all the publishers took a joint approach to help deal with the problems caused by the closure of the distributor. We worked together as an industry body.

There is much goodwill across our industry that sometimes baffles external people – when there is a passion for what you do, it sometimes transcends corporate boundaries.

Neil Morrison

secondary sources of information. Having strong relationships with organisations across and beyond their industries helped firms to gather vital insights during a time of unparalleled crisis and disruption.

Collaborative relationships are not just valuable in times of crisis. The interviews suggest that collaboration is an important means of helping firms to adapt to their markets. Forging strong relationships with customers was an important message, and, for some firms, close relationships with suppliers were also an important source of market intelligence and innovation. Other interviewees spoke of strategic alliances and joint ventures, and for firms that needed to keep abreast of advances in knowledge or technology, innovation-based partnerships were a priority.

Collaboration does not just entail close links with other organisations within or beyond a firm's industry. Those interviewed spoke of how a collaborative mindset helps keep individuals and the business as a whole open to new ways of thinking and encourages new ways of drawing in knowledge and insights.

Collaboration is now ubiquitous and takes many forms, including:

- informal co-operation;
- temporary alliances to share a limited set of skills or resources;

Wipro Infocrossing

We are part of a health-care manufacturing company. We take part in an active body of health-care manufacturers. We also have close links with a radiologists and cardiologists association. We became an active contributor to the discussions in these organisations about what was happening in the market and in terms of where technology is going and where our customers are heading.

This has proved a valuable source of information for us, particularly in terms of what may happen 10 years down the road, what is affordable for our customers and what market demand is likely to come from China and India.

Shivakumar Rajagopalin

- joint activity – such as joint marketing or joint manufacturing;
- equity investments;
- franchising;
- outsourcing;
- technology licensing;
- technology and know-how transfers, including technology development and university/industry research;
- research and development consortia;
- industry standard groups;
- innovation networks.

Firms use these different mechanisms as a way of adapting to intensifying competition and rapid change, often when moving into new sectors or new geographic markets; any international firm will have an emerging-market strategy that involves some form of collaboration. Indeed, in some emerging markets collaboration with local partners is obligatory. That apart, its advantages are that it helps local businesses:

Marsh

We need to ask what ideas and good practice are being discussed globally to enable us to foresee the future more accurately? What ideas are being developed from academia, consultancies and individual practitioners at the top of their game?

Daniel Galvao

- improve organisational operations and efficiencies;
- achieve economies of scale;
- obtain technology;
- gain access to specific markets;
- reduce financial risk or political risk;
- achieve or ensure competitive advantage;
- outsource non-core functions (as defined by an individual business – what is peripheral in one could be critical in another) such as customer service and human resources.

Some of these collaborations reduce risk and uncertainty, and firms should consider building a network of different types of partnerships to help them cope with and transcend uncertainty. For example, a firm can supplement gaps in its capabilities and know-how by teaming up with more specialist organisations. It can penetrate a new market by linking with a firm with intimate local knowledge. Instead of opting for a full-blown merger or acquisition, a strategic alliance or joint venture can help a firm gain a better sense of the potential benefits of a formal marriage or whether it is better just to work together.

Such collaborations depend on trust and mutual respect and the sharing of concerns and challenges as they move forward in an uncertain environment. Although difficult to maintain, these relationships are driven by the fact that the information and insights that are of most interest to the partners are not yet available as hard data and codified knowledge.

The nature of these collaborations can be as follows:

- **Internal,** connecting employees from different locations, markets, functions and technical backgrounds. This is often the starting point for helping staff to widen their thinking and more confidently confront whatever is unpredictable, uncontrollable and unknown in their work sphere.

- **External,** helping to build deeper and stronger relationships with customers. This type of collaboration aims at dissolving boundaries so that customers feel they "know" the business and can personally identify with its brand and corporate identity. Customers become willing to provide feedback and ideas and even participate in the co-creation of a product or service. Such a collaborative relationship has moved beyond well-designed marketing or customer service strategies – indeed, some customers can feel resentful if they seem to be treated like cogs in a well oiled marketing campaign.

- **Business-to-business** with strategic partners and suppliers.

- **Cross-industry** or "systems-wide", for example all the key players across a sector or system work together to solve a complex problem or predict (and try to shape) future events. The aim of this type of collaboration is to explore and collectively learn about issues and problems that are too complex for organisations to tackle on their own.

Today's firms have unprecedented opportunities to participate in or build such collaborative networks, not least because developments in telecommunications and technology convergence have made it far easier for organisations to work together and share information and knowledge. Businesses can expand their collaborative networks and forge links with a more diverse set of partners.

Internal collaboration

Terri Kelly, chief executive of W.L. Gore, says:[1]

> *Our young associates ... expect to have the chance to make an impact. They expect to know why they are working on something. They expect to work in a collaborative network where information*

is freely shared. If an organisation doesn't have these things, my suspicion is it won't be able to compete. You won't be able to attract the talent, and you certainly won't be able to retain it. This is what it's all about – getting the best brains together.

Many companies have taken on board how much can be gained from encouraging and enabling internal collaboration between employees from different functions or from different locations around the world. It makes it easier for the left hand to know what the right hand is doing and thereby avoid clashes and conflicts, it spurs innovation and it helps the business keep pace with a changing market. The point of collaboration is to enable an organisation to learn better and faster than its competitors.

Tools of collaboration

Advances in technology have enabled much greater internal collaboration through, for example, shared document drives and intranet pages, dashboards, blogs, instant messenger and business forums via tools like WebEx.

RBS, for example, values knowledge repository tools to help share knowledge. Diageo has sought to increase collaboration throughout its global organisation by recently creating 12 Halo sites (using HP's Halo technology) for more virtual meetings. Cisco's decentralised, committee-based structure is highly collaborative and depends heavily on a wide range of Web 2.0 technologies.

Many companies use ideas banks to enable employees to contribute ideas and creative thinking. These internal websites are particularly important for companies that need to keep producing a steady stream of improvements and innovation. Employees can post ideas or topics of interest to them, discuss these further with other enthusiasts, search for information or link with experts from other parts of the business.

Knowledge-management software allows companies to group ideas or topics together. These systems use algorithms to identify which issue or idea has the most views, "follows", bookmarks, comments or "alerts" or, if there is a voting system in place to help weight an idea or topic, the most votes.

China Telecom has used an internal ideas bank to help encourage and reward employees to think more creatively and collaboratively. Led by its Shanghai Research Institute, China Telecom worked with IBM, a US technology group, to create an initiative called "Innovation Works". All employees, not just those in R&D or product development, are encouraged to generate ideas for new service offerings or to improve existing ones. The company makes it clear that it is looking for not just the next best idea but also many small applications that can generate considerable value over time. An online social-media forum enables employees to post their ideas. Colleagues can respond and provide feedback, constructive criticism or practical advice about how the idea can be developed further. Some of the best ideas are entered in an annual internal innovation contest; some of these are then selected for development and may be successfully launched in the market.

Ideas banks can be an effective way of helping capture insights from staff across the business that might otherwise be lost. The potential behind one person's contribution can be picked up by someone in another part of the business and might then be taken up by more employees, discussed and gradually be developed.

Sharing company-wide data

Collaboration is also helped through the sharing of organisational data, especially around performance metrics and customer behaviour. With access to such data different parts of the business are better able to see and understand what they are achieving and need to work towards. However, the data should be used carefully. "Information can sometimes be used as a weapon," one interviewee said. "People can also feel very exposed – it can be like playing poker with all your cards showing." Management must keep everyone focused on the collective goals of the business and discourage any games of data politics.

Breaking down organisational boundaries

Another way to enable collaboration is to break down organisational boundaries so as to diminish territoriality between functions,

HCL Technologies

HCL Technologies, a leading offshore IT and software
development company, took the bold risk of opening "the
window of financial information" to all its employees.
The company believed that this would help create more
transparency, which would in turn create trust across the
business, and that more of its employees would contribute their
ideas and fresh thinking.

Anand Pillai, HCL's senior vice-president, describes this as
"beautiful involvement" and explains why it is important to the
company's success:[2]

*Approximately 80% of HCL Technologies' employees are
under 30 years of age. They have fresh ideas and no baggage,
no history to unlearn, no methods that are ingrained. When
business models change and the parameters of business success
shift, we need fresh thinking.*

departments, locations, and so on. This might be achieved through
adopting a project-based structure or simply by moving different
functions or departments closer to one another – perhaps in one
open-plan set-up.

These are just some of the ways firms break down silo thinking and
encourage an organisation to work more like a "collective brain". Each
part of the business can gain a better understanding of how it fits into
the whole. This can also help different parts of the business to make
difficult trade-offs, for example between short-term earning or future
growth. In terms of working within a diverse collaboration network, the
benefits are twofold: staff can build a more sophisticated understanding
of the complexities, tensions and conflicting pressures inherent in the
majority of international businesses; and this understanding will give
them some invaluable insights into the trade-offs and tensions that
inevitably surface between collaborative partners.

In terms of managing uncertainty, internal collaboration is most

Diageo and Ford

Diageo has put a lot of effort into integrating the IT function into the mainstream business by seeding IT staff across the consumer drinks company. The company is particularly keen for IT and marketing staff to work together to harness opportunities offered by emerging technologies.

This has resulted in several successful online campaigns for specific brands such as Smirnoff Vodka, the regular use of social-media sites such as Facebook and Twitter, and cocktail recipes that can be downloaded by customers to their mobile devices

Ford's more transparent reporting system has helped overcome internal fiefdoms and inculcate a sense of collective loyalty to the global business. Global divisional heads come together each week for a "Business Plan Review" based on detailed performance metrics.

Ford also stresses the importance of its vision and set of values around "One Ford, one company". It believes this has helped foster a collaborative culture where staff in different regions will put the global interests of the company before their regional priorities.

At the weekly review meeting, leaders bring one or two employees from their department to see how their role fits into the global business, and how their part of the business contributes to the success of the company. The aim is for these employees to take back this wider perspective to their departments.

powerful when employees are intellectually curious about their work and the wider environment. This requires them to reflect actively on their experiences and to keep questioning whether their experience and learning from the past are still relevant for success in the future. They need to continue this questioning with colleagues, even when this stirs up dissent or conflict.

None of this is easy. The pressure of day-to-day work is probably the biggest single barrier to personal reflection. Most people do not enjoy rocking the boat or confronting uncomfortable or complex questions about the future.

Business-to-business collaboration

It is really important for us to be alongside the customer, understanding the uncertainties that the customer is facing and then seeing if we can align ourselves to their business objectives as and when they change.

Can I as a company become a trusted adviser rather than simply a vendor – can I work with the customer to make them successful? I think a lot of our strategic assumptions are moving towards playing that role for example in the outcome-based, revenue-sharing models that we are now using.

We are saying that if you succeed then you pay me. So when we are in the same mess and the same quagmire we can support each other and move towards becoming successful.

Praful Pillay, SunGard India

Collaboration is now the norm for many international firms. However, in the quest for competitive advantage, businesses are looking to extract the highest possible value from their alliances and partnerships.

There is a marked shift towards less transactional and more relational arrangements as partners align their businesses to achieve mutually beneficial (although not necessarily identical) strategic goals. Exxon Chemical, for example, sponsored a conference on the future of customer-supplier relationships in the tyre industry in 2010, inviting its major customer, Goodyear, a tyre manufacturer, to participate in creating a strategic partnership.

Based on its 2009 study, *The Shape of Business: the Next 10 Years*, the Confederation of British Industry (CBI) says that the financial crisis and continuing economic turbulence have accelerated the move from transactional to collaborative relationships. The study revealed that many international companies have been forced to rethink their business structures.

W.L. Gore

W.L. Gore is known for its Gore-Tex range of high-performance fabrics. It employs 9,000 staff in 50 locations around the world. In 2010, Gary Hamel hailed the company as one of the most innovative in the world because of its success in abolishing a hierarchical structure for a "lattice" or network model.

Employees work flexibly in self-organising teams that are formed for temporary projects and then disbanded. Collaboration is a crucial means of ensuring the success of the network. Employees are required to be self-driven and choose for themselves which projects to join in order to make the biggest contribution to the company's success. There is no traditional management hierarchy. Leaders are expected to emerge naturally and their talent is then confirmed by whether or not other employees elect to follow them.

Project teams are cross-functional. The company works hard to demolish internal boundaries because it believes this damages innovation. Sales, manufacturing and research teams work in the same place so they can pool their expertise and find the best solution or outcome. W.L. Gore has also built business campuses in diverse locations such as the United States, Germany and China, which enables it to co-locate a diverse set of businesses and factories.

The company strongly believes that its long-established track record in innovation stems from its commitment to collaboration. Each employee is expected to collaborate and share knowledge.

In the light of a more challenging and uncertain global environment, companies are looking for ways of becoming more flexible, more collaborative and leaner. The CBI report predicts the following:

The need to share risk, invest effectively in developing new innovations, and access finance and competencies will drive

Each member of staff ("associate") is ranked by 20 or so colleagues. Rankings are based on both the contribution to the team and the broader impact across the company, especially in terms of collaborative behaviour. The company believes this unstructured model works effectively because it has well-embedded values in terms of encouraging individuals and fostering a "collaborative spirit" and knowledge sharing.

W.L. Gore's chief executive, Terri Kelly, comments about the importance of building strong and trusting relationships across the business:[3]

> Some of the most "impactful" decisions are made by small teams. Within any team you'll find people with very different perspectives; they don't think alike – and we encourage this. We encourage teams to take a lot of time to come together, to build trust, to build relationships, because we know that if you throw them into a room and they don't have a foundation of trust, it will be chaotic, it will be political and people will feel as if they are being personally attacked.
>
> We invest a lot of time in making our teams effective, so when they have those great debates – where a scientist doesn't agree with a sales associate ... – the debate happens in an environment where everyone is looking for a better solution, versus "you win, I lose".

businesses to a more collaborative business model over the next five to ten years. The shift from transactional to collaborative relationships will bring about new alliances with a wide range of partners – establishing and maintaining trust will be critical.

Research by KPMG, a global consultancy firm, in 2011 also reveals a trend towards closer, more collaborative relationships. The company's report, based on a questionnaire of UK-based international businesses, the perspective of subject experts, business case studies and an analysis of trends in Europe, the Middle East and Africa, looked at trends in outsourcing and offshoring projects.

The report concludes that companies are working more closely with a smaller number of outsourcing service providers. Companies were initially driven by the need for cost reduction during the financial crisis and economic downturn in various parts of the world, but their focus has now broadened. Cost reduction is still important but "speed and flexibility are joining cost saving as key requirements". Outsourcers are also seeking innovation from their service providers.

Bill Thomas, CEO and senior partner at KPMG (UK), describes the shift towards relational collaboration:[4]

> *Relationships between service provider and customer are maturing – there is a greater appreciation of the fact that a collaborative relationship is a more effective strategy than simply squeezing the service provider to reduce costs. As a result of this thinking, we increasingly see companies having a smaller portfolio of service providers, allowing them to have more time to maintain and improve relationships with their outsourcing partners.*

The research by KPMG and the CBI suggests that technology-based change is a major driver of closer collaboration. The pace of technological innovation as well as the adoption and convergence of new technologies mean that companies need to adapt rapidly to take advantage of the opportunities that arise. For example, the CBI study points to the rise of digital technologies, "the use of which has fundamentally changed business models and the behaviour and expectations of individual consumers and businesses over the last decade". It cites research by comScore that shows that 113 billion internet searches were conducted in July 2009, an increase of 41% compared with July 2008.

Innovation-based collaborations are a particularly effective means of tackling uncertainty head on. For example, companies with enough clout and resources can use partnerships to advance new technologies. NASA's Innovative Partnership Programme does just this, working with numerous entrepreneurial firms around the world to ensure it can meet critical needs for future missions. The agency's Glenn Research Centre has, for example, forged a successful partnership with Goodyear to develop non-pneumatic tyres for use on the Moon and eventually Mars.

In other cases, firms use innovative partnerships to create a new market. Samsung's strategy for 3D TV, announced in 2010, is to create a market for this technology by working in partnership with companies such as DreamWorks Animation (which produces animated films, television programmes and online virtual worlds) and Technicolor (the world's largest film processor and the largest independent manufacturer and distributor of DVDs, including Blu-ray). By working with these partners, Samsung hopes to stimulate 3D content and create a "new entertainment experience", in the words of Tim Baxter, president, Samsung Electronics America.

Pharmaceutical firms are using partnerships to reinvent themselves as their most profitable medicines go off patent and uncertainty around replacement drugs increases. Large companies such as Merck and AstraZeneca have depended on a small number of high-priced, mass-market "blockbusters" to create billions of dollars a year in sales. But as patents on these drugs expire, the industry is rethinking its business model. In recent years there has been a huge increase in collaborative ventures between pharmaceutical firms and small biotech firms.

Large global firms are also working together to bring new medicines to the market faster. For example, GlaxoSmithKline has spun off its HIV work entirely into ViiV Healthcare, a joint venture with Pfizer. This has enabled both companies to share the expertise, costs and benefits of new product development.

Technology firms are turning to their suppliers for innovation. Supplier firms are doing increasingly high-value work where their more entrepreneurial capabilities can have full expression. These arrangements exploit the flexibility of smaller entrepreneurial businesses that are able to adjust to changes in economic circumstances.

Apple, for example, has always used niche firms to develop applications for its iPhone. However, Google has taken an alternative path by using open-source software that enables external parties

Best Buy

Best Buy, a large American electronics retailer, has pursued a strategy of collaborating with electronics manufacturers such as Hewlett-Packard, Sony Electronics and Toshiba. The company's collaborative strategy is aligned to a fast-moving, highly competitive industry. It has chosen to use its clout and influence (it has over 1,000 stores in the United States) to shape its competitive space by becoming a hybrid retail/technology company and by influencing emerging technologies.

Best Buy sends senior staff to manufacturers' factories to influence product design and development. It is pushing for its own preferred solutions, such as persuading manufacturers to standardise their software and digital services. It has also created a venture-capital fund to invest in technology start-ups around the world. "We are talking to players deep into engineering the future," was how Best Buy's former chief executive, Brian J. Dunn, explained the move to investors and analysts in 2009.

Best Buy has introduced its own brands such as Next Class and Blue Label, which consist of exclusive products that have been manufactured by partners such as HP, Sony and Toshiba, but with design features based on customer feedback from Best Buy's consumer forum programme, "You spoke, we listened". The programme has also helped manufacturers take a new direction – for example, Toshiba worked with Best Buy to launch in 2010 its first laptop designed exclusively for children aged between five and ten.

However, Bloomberg *Businessweek*, an American publication, suggests that some manufacturers are uneasy about the balance

to develop applications. Google's decision to opt for open-source software in its Android operating system has been a spectacular success, with some 28 Android-based handsets now launched on the market.

As KMPG's 2011 outsourcing study reveals, outsourcing companies

of power between themselves and Best Buy. According to
Businessweek:[5]

> *Executives at several major consumer electronics companies*
> *worry privately about Best Buy's growing influence. They're*
> *concerned that Dunn and his team could block them from getting*
> *innovative products in front of customers or favour Best Buy*
> *backed goods over their own.*

It goes on to cite the executive of a company that sells
televisions and other products to Best Buy: "We used to call them
the 800-pound gorilla. Now with a lot of competition gone,
they're the 1,000-pound gorilla."

Best Buy's strategy has proven effective at beating other retail
businesses. However, it may not be enough to see off competition
from online retailers. Analysts have expressed concern that Best
Buy's stores are serving as a showcase for online rivals such as
Amazon, with customers viewing products at Best Buy's stores
but purchasing online. Best Buy's performance has spiralled
downwards as a result of online competition and internal
problems such as inventory management and customer service –
as well as the sudden departure in April 2012 of its chief executive
and in June 2012 of its founder and chairman following an
internal investigation into the alleged personal misconduct of the
CEO. As the share price fell, the original founder launched a bid
for the company.

are moving swiftly up the value chain to become trusted partners.
Vineet Nayar, chief executive of HCL Technologies, sums up this new
relationship:[6]

In a knowledge economy, we want customers to be transparent with us, to share their ideas, their visions for the future, and their strategies for solving core problems. Without such transparency, how can we create the technology solutions that will accelerate their growth and strengthen their businesses?

Indian outsourcing companies are doing particularly well in this area: according to the *Financial Times*, India's top three outsourcers have achieved impressive growth.[7] Tata Consultancy, the industry leader based on revenue, saw its sales increase by more than 20% between January 2011 and January 2012. The other two leading outsourcers, Infosys and Wipro, achieved an approximately 15% increase in sales in the same period.

Some of this advance has been helped by the arrival of cloud computing and mobile devices, which together enable outsourcers to create myriad new services for their customers. Another reason is the different way they are now working with their corporate customers. The new emphasis is on business development on a much wider scale rather than operational efficiencies. For example, with the aim of launching a new vaccine for swine flu as swiftly as possible, Sanofi Pasteur (the vaccines division of Sanofi Group, a French multinational pharmaceutical company) used Cognizant, a US-based outsourcer, to run 30 large clinical trials using teams based in France, the United States and India.

However, the move to closer, more collaborative relationships between buyers and their suppliers is not without problems. There is always a risk of tension between co-operation and competition when rival companies collaborate. There can also be tension between exploration and exploitation. The resource-richer company (for example, in terms of revenue, influence or access to market) may be tempted to build what is known as an "asymmetrical" partnership, where the benefits of collaboration swing gradually towards the more dominant partner. If not managed properly, these tensions will lead to a loss of trust and openness and the collaboration will not achieve what it was intended to.

Best Buy is not the only company to juggle with the complexities of moving to a new collaborative relationship with suppliers. The

KPMG study also found that outsourcing companies and their clients struggled to gain the full value from a closer relationship. Companies and outsourcing partners were asked about their experiences of working together to generate more innovative solutions. The study found that while both parties took innovation seriously, "they reached an impasse on how to manage it, fund it, and ultimately turn it into a reality".

The research flagged up three ways to create more value in the collaboration, all of which hinged on improving the relationship. Recommendations included the following:[8]

■ Both parties should put more effort into investigating the challenges facing the buyer and exploring how they can be tackled.

■ The provider should share with the buyer any relevant experiences it has had with other clients.

■ The buyer should give the provider more access to stakeholders, particularly sponsors from the business.

■ Both parties should put equivalent resources into their joint efforts to develop an innovative and effective approach.

Collaborative relationships can be complex and difficult to manage. What matters is that the parties take time to understand each other's operations and strategic plans. They have to establish mutual respect, even when one partner has far more resources or capabilities than the other. And they have to pursue mutual benefit and not be intensely exploitative.

Collaboration with customers

Managing uncertainty is about being market oriented and market focused so that when things are uncertain you look at your customers and really understand what is going on. If you are relying on middlemen to translate it for you, you already have one degree of separation and that means time slips away.

We want direct relationships with consumers, through such means as focus groups, online consumer insight tools such as online panels, and questionnaires and social media.

Burberry

Burberry, a British fashion company, has revitalised itself through its relaunch and reinvention of its most iconic garment, the trench coat. It decided to connect with younger, more digitally savvy customers by launching a social-media platform called "Art of the Trench". Photographers and trench-coat owners are invited to participate and the best of the submitted shots are added to the site. Users can comment on and share photos, and the site links directly to Facebook.

Angela Ahrendts, Burberry's chief executive, spoke of the importance of using social media to connect with a new generation of customers. During discussion on leadership after the financial crisis she commented:[9]

The Art of the Trench allowed us to introduce the thing that we do best in the world, and have for years, to a whole new young generation of consumers who might think [the trench coat] is just something that Dad wears. So our goal is to connect constantly and remind everybody that that's what we do, that's what we're the best at.

Social-media analytics are very important; they help you understand what the noise is around certain subjects before events that might help you identify publishing opportunities. It could be talking to bloggers who blog in a certain sector on which we publish. It could be using social media to talk to people – it is just being very curious and focused on what the consumer is interested in and why.

Neil Morrison, Random House

The tricky thing now is to work out what shape that relationship should take and how best to achieve it.

Engaging with customers: dialogue and interaction

Social media enable companies to engage with customers and social networks such as Facebook, Twitter, LinkedIn, My Space and YouTube help companies obtain feedback and ideas from customers and, more importantly, engage them in a genuine dialogue.

There is scant tolerance for clumsy marketing campaigns or heavy-handed selling techniques. Companies have to respect their customers' virtual "space" and entice them in through initiatives that are important to them, interesting or fun to participate in. Humility, respect and creativity are the essential qualities for any firm wanting to engage customers.

The success of Burberry's "Art of the Trench" initiative shows how social media can enable a company to re-energise its brand and directly connect with a new generation of customers (see example). Nike came up with the popular idea of putting sensors in its shoes to enable runners to monitor their performance. Customers can visit a web platform to chat and exchange their running data with other enthusiasts.

Co-creation

The concept of co-creation was originally introduced by C.K. Prahalad and Venkat Ramaswamy, two business school professors, in 2000 and further expounded in their book *The Future of Competition*.[10] It hinges on the recognition that the creation of value no longer resides within the confines of the corporation. If companies want to compete in an increasingly global and interconnected world, they have to create value with their customers. They accomplish this through working alongside consumers and customers to develop products. Co-creation also enables customers to shape their own experience of the product or service.

Co-creation is used to improve the customer experience and to discover emerging customer tastes, needs and preferences. Harley Davidson, an American motorcycle manufacturer, for example, works with customers on customising their motorcycles. Small entrepreneurial businesses can also directly link with customers online. For example, Bobsmade, an online business run by young

German artists, enables a customer to suggest a theme or concept which is then developed by the artists to personalise a product for the customer such as shoes, spectacles, headphones and iPhone cases.

Companies also collaborate with customers to develop new offerings. For example, Unilever first used co-creation in designing its 2010 variant of the Lynx/Axe deodorant. Young men from its target audience in the United States, Germany and the UK worked with the company's perfume experts and advertising staff. The team worked on the concept of "fresh" to develop a scent, brand name, packaging design and advertising strategy for the new co-created product.

Crowd sourcing

This is another way for companies to "mass collaborate" with their customers. Pioneered by Jeff Howe, crowd sourcing involves an "open call" via the internet inviting interested parties to collaborate to solve a complex problem or contribute fresh ideas on a specific issue. This can open a window on the future and lead companies into new areas of thinking or inquiry. Nokia, for example, used crowd sourcing to look at the concept, future use and functionality of its next generation of handsets. It engaged a number of technology leaders to explore the problems and shortcomings of its existing smartphones. It then got them to take part in a two-day workshop, where they worked with the company's designers and design researchers.

Such new forms of collaboration are spreading rapidly as companies try to anticipate how their markets will evolve over the next few years. It requires companies to be open and transparent about their thinking, especially in terms of future direction and strategic priorities, and also to be willing to shed assumptions that they are the experts or that they can control the collaborative process.

Francis Gouillart, president of the Experience Co-Creation Partnership, a management education and consulting firm in Massachusetts, does not think that organisations are ready for this transformation. Despite the fact that companies now have countless opportunities to develop different forms of "interactive platforms" with customers via their products, physical sites and online sites, they continue to stick to the old ways. He comments:

Most product development groups continue to design non-interactive products. Company people in call centres and company stores still generally follow company narratives. Most corporate IT departments and suppliers are trained in one-way project-management techniques incompatible with true engagement-platform development.

Gouillart has recently co-authored a book on co-creation with Venkat Ramaswamy.[11] They argue that co-creation is a more "inclusive, meaningful, creative and transformative" way of working for all concerned. They stress the need for four essential ingredients:

- high-quality dialogue between co-creators, so there can be a rich interaction and exchange of ideas and insights;
- transparency of interactive platforms, so everyone can contribute to the process;
- access to and expertise in knowledge-management tools so all the co-creators can mine and share creativity;
- reflexivity, where co-creators have the tools to bring their ideas and solutions back to the interaction platform so "something new is created".

Cross-industry or system-wide collaboration

We work with legislators and we have regular dialogue with both the regulators and the individual politicians. We are going down the road of working with politicians who want to work with us and who are supporting the banking industry.

We have a good relationship with individual Congressmen. We can try to leverage this. Equally we are trying to stay close to our clients. It is very important that we work closely with our clients and are responsive to their needs – that's how we get paid.

Iain Worsley, Capital One Bank

Horizontal collaborations are increasingly helping businesses to collaborate with partners from different industries and public-sector or other not-for-profit organisations. Such collaborations connect organisations that have different experiences and capabilities, but which share the common goal of wanting to combine their thinking about an issue of mutual concern.

At one end of the spectrum are open innovation collaborations between industry and academia. Open innovation involves organisations sharing their resources, ideas and expertise. GlaxoSmithKline announced in 2010 the development of a £170m biotech science park in the UK in an effort to create a life sciences cluster around Cambridge and the east of England to rival the leading American centres of Boston and North Carolina. Called the Stevenage Bioscience Catalyst (SBC), the new campus is a joint venture between the UK government's Department for Business, Innovation and Skills, GlaxoSmithKline, the Wellcome Trust, the East of England Development Agency and the Technology Strategy Board. SBC opened for business at the start of 2012. The first wave of "tenants" include Aptiv Solutions, which specialises in clinical trials for biopharmaceutical and medical devices, and a new Centre for Innovation established by Cambridge University, which aims to work in partnership with other firms at SBC to create new medicines.

Nokia Research Centre is engaging in open innovation with world-leading institutions such as Beijing University of Posts and Telecommunications (BUPT), Helsinki University of Technology, Cambridge University and the Massachusetts Institute of Technology. The centre's focused research is on the experiences people will have in the future, the technology and interfaces they will use, and the infrastructure required to help these innovations become a reality.

Cross-industry, cross-sector and international collaborative networks are another way for firms to tap into many diverse perspectives. Membership is a valuable means of helping increase a business's awareness of events in far-flung corners of the world that might become major sources of uncertainty or disruption. These networks can also provide warnings about hidden problems, such as corruption, security threats or problems with supply chain partners that are failing to comply with international standards.

Some of these "horizontal" collaborations are led by governments, and it is likely that such networks will proliferate. The financial crisis was a sharp reminder of the interconnected nature of national financial systems and economies.

Open collaboration: an emergent capability

It is clear that in an uncertain environment, businesses (whether large or small, local or global) need to have a collaborative mindset and seek partners with whom they can form productive partnerships. Such relationships can act as an antenna, helping a business to sense different manifestations of uncertainty: disruptive and unpredictable events, unforeseen risk, sudden connections between previously unrelated trends, a local event or problem that causes a ripple effect across the wider business environment.

A collaborative network may be more difficult to manage but is potentially more valuable than just one or two partnerships. This is partly because of the diversity of perspectives and experiences that a network offers, but also because of the flexibility and agility that such a portfolio allows. Each form of collaboration has the potential to uncover useful information that may be invisible to any outside individual or organisation.

In response to uncertainty, firms need to move towards "open collaboration" and to building relationships with partners that in a spirit of exploration, openness and mutual curiosity enable them to pool their experiences and learn from each other. In doing so they can examine the "white noise" of the external environment and peer beyond the boundaries of their expertise to debate "known unknowns" and "unknown unknowns". Ambiguity, contradiction and confusion are viewed as invitations for further exploration, rather than something to be shied away from.

Collaborators must seek to harness diversity and view any conflict as part of the process of exploration – something to be used rather than ignored or closed down. What is perhaps most important is the recognition that it is their combined diversity that will help them gain a broader perspective of what their environment might look like in the future.

In contrast, "closed collaboration" is a form of collaboration that is probably more suited to a stable environment, focusing on what is known or predictable and therefore controlled and measured. In a closed collaboration, the organisation initiating the partnership often expects to be the locus of control. It specifies the terms of the collaboration, the processes and procedures, and the expected or desired inputs and outputs of all the partners. In this model, the emphasis is on compliance, meeting quality-control specifications or contractually based agreements, and tangible, measurable outcomes. There are clear boundaries between partners and up-front agreements about what resources and capabilities should be shared.

In moving towards open collaboration, firms must:

- **Create an open and enquiring culture.** Encourage staff to be curious about their work, question the status quo and participate in dissent, conflict and debate, share emergent learning in the shape of hunches, intuition, fresh thinking and innovative ideas. Increase opportunities for different parts of the organisation to link together, both formally (such as through "search conferences" that are specifically designed to help participants identify future trends) and informally (for example, through intranet sites).

- **Make good use of information technology.** This might be through shared document drives, intranet pages, online communities and networks, wikis and other collaborative sites, blogging and online storytelling, online webinars and virtual meetings. IT should be used not only to encourage learning, creativity and innovation, but also with the explicit purpose of creating valuable links that enable knowledge and expertise to be shared.

- **Capture and make better use of knowledge.** Put in place systems for the capture and codification and management of knowledge, for example through the use of knowledge repository tools, such as databases and book-marking engines, and tools that disseminate best practice. Other measures that can be considered are post-project evaluations, action learning and bringing people together to share their experiences, insights and knowledge.

- **Build the capability.** This involves creating a shared understanding of the advantages of linking with external organisations and the identification of the criteria, processes and so on to be used for different types of collaboration. This will of

course involve learning from existing partnerships and from the
experiences of other organisations.

■ **Develop a network.** Start small and expand gradually, perhaps
to include anything from professional link-ups to formal
collaborations within an industry. Investigate opportunities for
staff to meet partners formally and informally, through site visits,
work shadowing, short-term secondments and membership of
temporary task-forces.

■ **Have managers who are good at collaborative working.**
Performance-management processes should be designed to
help managers develop collaborative expertise, and managers
involved in collaborations must act as ambassadors and
evangelists for the business imperative of such partnerships.

GlaxoSmithKline's strategy of "externalisation"

GlaxoSmithKline (GSK) is a leading research-based pharmaceutical
company, employing approximately 99,000 employees in 100
countries. Since 2008, the company has been transforming its
business model by reducing its internal research and development
(R&D) to pursue a strategy of "externalisation" with a number of
different collaborative partners.

Adrian Rawcliffe, senior vice-president, worldwide business
development for R&D, explains how externalisation helps GSK
manage uncertainty:

> *If I think about uncertainty and R&D ... the most interesting question
> is how do you shape the front end of your investment in R&D in
> an environment where your product cycle time is 10–15 years but
> the pace of change in certain areas is so fast that it's a lot shorter
> than your product cycle time? How do we identify and capitalise
> on the disruptive things that happen out there and that relate very
> closely to how we manage our alliances? That's the purpose of our
> externalisation strategy.*

GSK's externalisation strategy helps it to manage uncertainty in
two ways. In terms of innovation, multiple forms of collaboration
help the company "place bets on things that have a low probability of

success but a high upside", says Rawcliffe. But external collaboration also helps GSK gain "optionality on business models". Rawcliffe explains:

> It is much easier to experiment with different models through our partnerships than it is to experiment with creating business models internally ... so from a scientific and business model approach, our strategy of alliances works well in managing uncertainty.

GSK has different forms of collaboration that cover a drug's life stage from discovery through to development. The company has fundamentally changed its R&D approach, directing most of its expenditure to late-stage drug development. It now has a diverse portfolio of approximately 30 "opportunities" in vaccines, biopharmaceuticals and pharmaceuticals. A large proportion of its late-stage pipeline is the result of collaborations via late-stage licensing.

GSK has drastically overhauled its drug discovery activities, reducing internal activity in favour of external collaboration and streamlining its portfolio. It has terminated projects with low financial and scientific returns in favour of products that are likely to deliver a 14% return on investment in R&D.

The company looks for the best opportunities in its chosen specialist areas and seeks to marry its expertise with external partners that are leaders in their field. For example, GSK Oncology is collaborating with more than 160 cancer centres around the world. These collaborations range from shared research through to more formal "option-based" ones. This is where GSK works with a partner to bring a promising idea to the stage of "clinical proof of concept", at which point it has the option of in-licensing, where the programme is taken in-house for further development and commercialisation.

There is much collaboration with academia, for example with Harvard Stem Cell Institute and the Immune Disease Institute in Boston. As noted above, GSK has also headed the development of a biotech science park adjoining its research base in Stevenage in the UK. It aims to help extend the technology cluster further across eastern England. It also hopes to promote innovative start-ups and help them gain commercial benefits from their science. There is open innovation at the science park to allow the early-stage companies better access to GSK's work and also to link them into broader science networks across the technology cluster.

Collaboration now takes place in all shapes and forms. "We are absolutely committed to finding talent, ideas, technologies and new medicines outside of GSK," says Rawcliffe.

However, GSK had to undergo a profound shift over a number of years in its mindset and culture to embed collaborative working. One important step was to reward R&D staff on the basis of their outputs. Rawcliffe explains:

> As soon as you focus on output-based activity and you make money available for partnering, then people change as they realise it is in their interest to look outside GSK to see what is out there that could help or disrupt their pipeline ... If they needed to make a trade-off between an internal or external asset, people started to pick the one that had the best chance of success, not the one they had personally activated. Now we have 55 alliances for early-stage drug development and the large majority were selected by people fairly low in the organisation.

Another important step was to "re-personalise" R&D by creating smaller, more accountable R&D teams. The idea is to empower teams and to give them the freedom to work as collaboratively as possible. Rawcliffe comments:

> Rather than decisions being taken by five or six people at the very top of the company and then imposing these on everyone else, we are encouraging everybody close to the coalface to comprehend that the only way they are going to be successful is if they understand the external environment and are able to exploit it effectively – and therefore they start taking key decisions.

GSK has created some 40 Discovery Performance Units, made up of 5–70 scientists. Each group focuses on a particular disease or clinical pathway and is responsible for driving the discovery and development of potential new medicines. They can seek help in alliance management from the company's Alliance Management Centre of Excellence, which provides trained staff to collaborative partnerships as they come on stream. The centre also provides standardised processes based on best practice, and training and development in alliance management.

GSK now has a clear "externalisation" strategy for R&D and the structures in place to enable many different forms of collaboration. Embedding a genuinely collaborative culture is a longer-term challenge and something that needs constant attention, according to Letizia Amadini-Lane, head of R&D leadership culture:

> *If you are moving from a situation where your products are being developed internally to one where they are in part dependent on external alliances, you need to pay close attention to the attitudes of your people. This task is not a one-off; it is a constant. You are never done doing it. You need to pay attention and tune in all the time. You have to go into the belly of the organisation, you need to engage, you need to learn, you need to listen ... Admitting that there may be better solutions outside the company is not easy for us. Flexible thinking and a little humility are required to make this work – and this is something we need to keep looking at.*

7 Predictive learning

The capability to sense, probe and analyse previously hidden patterns and trends in order to anticipate sudden or disruptive change

> *You have to get signals from the market beamed back to the organisation as purely as possible and try to keep those signals from being distorted.*
>
> Eric Beinhocker, *The Origin of Wealth*

ACCORDING TO RAINER FEURER, senior vice-president, corporate strategy and planning environment at BMW, the quality of any organisation's strategy depends on the quality of knowledge it draws on (see Chapter 2). This in turn hinges on how effectively the process of knowledge gaining is managed in the organisation. Strategy formulation, Feurer stressed, must therefore be regarded as a constant learning process and the quality of strategy directly depends on the quality of an organisation's cognitive and behavioural learning mechanisms.

For GlaxoSmithKline, learning about an uncertain environment is an unstructured and informal process that occurs when staff are naturally curious and inquiring. The company has a deep foundation of scientific inquiry, but it is critical that its staff look outside the organisation and tap into fresh ideas and perspectives. Adrian Rawcliffe explains:

> *I do think that there are organisational capabilities around business intelligence that one can point to, as well as companies with excellent and relevant "baked in" business intelligence. These companies have a systematic process. They have determined what things they need*

to be paying attention to and they have worked out ways to get hold of that information and disseminate it around the organisation very effectively.

But the best business intelligence capabilities will only tell you about the "known" stuff. What they will miss and where there is no substitute for intuition, is the "unknown" stuff, because you can't set up a system to gather this. It is about what the top 500 people in a large company pay attention to and how wide they see their role. What external boards are they on? What are they reading? How much time are they spending outside GSK thinking about the external environment?

Rawcliffe points out that this type of external sensing should ideally occur throughout the organisation – "a lot of it is about people's mindset", he says.

In contrast to GSK's emphasis on informal processes, RBS (see Chapter 3) has looked backwards in order to prepare for an uncertain future. One of the most important ways in which RBS attempted to reform its operations in the wake of its very public crash in 2009 was to capture and codify the experience of its surviving executives so that this could be learned from in the future. It used a variety of knowledge-management technology and tools developed in conjunction with Accenture, a consulting firm.

As Donna Hamilton, RBS's head of group learning, says:

After every strategy execution, whether successful or not, we need to stop and think about what made that execution successful or not, capture that learning and share it and refer back to it.

At a very simple level it is about doing project evaluation reviews and always considering what happened last time. I think we are becoming much better as an organisation at systematically capturing data that can be codified and referred to the next time so that it is all there and waiting.

There is always the challenge that people move on and change roles before the lessons have been learned and stored and we are seeking ways to stop this happening.

Predictive learning is therefore critical to organisations' ability to manage uncertainty – in the sense that it enables senior executives to sense, probe and analyse hidden patterns and trends in order to anticipate sudden or disruptive change.

Getting better at predictive learning involves making use of:

- analytics, including data mining;
- double-loop learning;
- abduction.

Analytics

According to Accenture's Institute for High Performance Business, analytics is "the extensive use of data, statistical and quantitative analysis, explanatory and predictive models, and fact-based management to drive decisions and actions".[1] Analytics may be applied to almost any aspect of business, including customer or supply chain management and financial performance.

Chapter 2 showed how Capital One Bank's opportunistic acquisition of Chevy Chase Bank in 2008 was facilitated by senior executives' ability to sift accurately market analysis from independent experts, strategic partners and suppliers.

The ability to analyse and interpret accurately the data accumulated by an organisation is seen by Eric Beinhocker of the McKinsey Global Institute as essential if senior executives are to anticipate and respond to sudden opportunities or threats. As he says:

> Years ago, one client of mine described the process as being like funhouse mirrors – the signals come in from the market and they bounce around and twist and by the time the intelligence reaches the CEO suite it doesn't look anything like the original.
>
> People have interests in their business succeeding and that their pet projects are preserved. So you have to create mechanisms that make sure that you have very good intelligence coming in and can make those selection decisions and that it is as rigorous and fact based and undistorted as possible.
>
> What continually surprises me is how that information gets boiled down into a handful of financial figures that are often quite spurious. What you really want to know about is the customer

survey data, relationships with suppliers, what outside experts might be saying – that is a much more contextual, multidimensional view of what your market is telling you.

Two experts on analytics are Tom Davenport, President's Chair in Information Technology and Management at Babson College, and Jeanne Harris, executive research fellow and senior executive at the Accenture Institute for High Performance Business. They are the authors of *Competing on Analytics: The New Science of Winning* and the more recent *Analytics at Work: Smarter Decisions, Better Results* (with Robert Morison). Their central argument is that high-performance businesses use analytics for competitive differentiation.

They explain that analytics can be current and predictive. They define "descriptive analytics" as "the what". This form of analysis describes what happened in the past through reports, "queries, drill downs, and alerts". Predictive analytics uses data to understand the "so what". This form of analysis, which includes forecasting, predictive modelling and optimisation, is focused on the future.

Davenport and Harris argue:[2]

The use of predictive analytics takes an organisation to a higher degree of intelligence and can yield competitive advantage. Analytics' potential contribution is great, especially in light of exciting advances in behavioural economics, neurobiology, artificial intelligence, and even "the wisdom of crowds".

They also comment:[3]

True competitive advantage comes when organisations apply analytics across the enterprise, as opposed to applying it only to segments of the organisation. More companies will choose to compete on analytics as their distinctive capability in the next five years as a way to outperform their competitors.

Davenport and Harris divide an organisation's analytical capability into five stages:

- Stage 1: Analytically impaired ("flying blind").

- Stage 2: Localised analytics (isolated, fragmented, disconnected, inconsistent, etc).
- Stage 3: Analytical aspirations (sees need, begins to explore options).
- Stage 4: Analytical companies (enterprise-wide perspective, eager to innovate and differentiate).
- Stage 5: Analytical competitors (analytics is the primary driver of performance and value).

According to Davenport and Harris, companies are becoming more analytically mature and are developing greater analytical capabilities, but overall, progress has been slow.

They comment:

> When companies compete based on analytics, analytics is having a positive bottom-line impact. However, for all its potential, analytics is not yet having a major impact on the quality of corporate decision-making. This is the untapped potential: using analytical capabilities, culture, and processes to make better decisions.

This insight has been confirmed by research by IBM Institute for Business Value in association with *MIT Sloan Management Review*.[4] In 2010, the two organisations conducted a survey of nearly 3,000 executives, managers and analysts working in more than 30 industries across 100 countries. The research suggested that organisations have access to unprecedented amounts of information but senior leaders are struggling to know how to "obtain value" from their data. They also struggle to know if they are "correctly interpreting new signals from the global economy and adequately assessing the impact on their customers and partners".

According to the study, there is a clear link between performance and the competitive value of analytics. Based on self-assessment by respondents, the top-performing organisations use analytics five times more than the lower performers. They approached analytics differently, for example:

- they put analytics to use "in the widest possible range of decisions, large or small";

- they were twice as likely to use analytics to guide future strategies;
- they were twice as likely to use analytics to guide day-to-day operations;
- they made decisions "based on rigorous analysis" at more than double the rate of lower performers.

The study identifies three levels of capabilities among respondents:

- Level 1: "Aspirational", where the focus is to use analytics to increase efficiency or cut costs.
- Level 2: "Experienced", where the focus is to go beyond cost efficiencies and find ways to collect and act on analytics to optimise the organisation.
- Level 3: "Transformed", where the focus is to use analytics as a competitive differentiator. Analytics is used across a broad range of functions and helps "drive customer profitability".

Common barriers to using analytics effectively include "lack of management bandwidth due to competing priorities" (cited by one in three respondents) and a general lack of understanding "of how to use analytics to improve the business" (according to almost four out of ten respondents). Half the respondents said improving information and analytics was a top priority in their organisations. One in five said they were "under intense or significant pressure to adopt advanced information and analytics approaches".

The IBM survey reveals that gaining capability in analytics is critical:

> Knowing what happened and why it happened are no longer adequate. Organisations need to know what is happening now, what is likely to happen next, and what action should be taken to get the optimal results.

Using analytics effectively

The main purpose of effective analytics, as Beinhocker explains above, is to pick up market signals early and accurately. According to Palo Alto's Institute for the Future (IFTF), a non-profit research centre, a signal might be a new product, a new practice, a new market strategy, a new policy or a new technology. It can be an event, a local trend, or a new competitor. It can also be a recently revealed problem or state of affairs. In short, it is something, as the IFTF puts it, "that catches our attention at one scale and in one locale and points to larger implications for other locales or even globally".

As the IFTF goes on to explain:[5]

Signals are useful for people who are trying to anticipate a highly uncertain future. They tend to capture emergent phenomena sooner than traditional science methods.

Unlike trends, they turn our attention to possible innovations before they become obvious. Unlike indicators, they often focus our attention on the margins of society rather than the core.

In this way, they are more likely to reveal disruptions and innovations. Of course, local trends and indicators can function as signals: when a trend hits a certain threshold, for example, it might be a signal of a change in the larger population, as when an innovation moves beyond a lead user stage and begins to diffuse much more rapidly.

Data mining and categorisation

In Chapter 2, Phiroz Bhagat, the author of *Pattern Recognition in Industry*, described how pattern recognition can enable senior executives to pick "meaning" out of the huge quantity of information they receive about the business environment in which they operate. This encompasses social, economic and political trends as well as the market, including developments, the initiatives of competitors, and the current state of stakeholders such as partners and strategic partners.

Bhagat argues that firms can avoid being overwhelmed by the enormous amount of data they receive through the way they "mine" and "categorise" it:

The main task is to differentiate between data and information and between information and knowledge. Once you get the idea of the differences between them, you can in a methodological way categorise the data you are receiving ... For a couple of decades, I worked for a very large operation and the whole focus of the organisation was devoted to trying to extract the right data that they needed to make informed strategic decisions.

Generally, data mining (sometimes called data or knowledge discovery) is the process of analysing data from different perspectives and summarising it into useful information, which can be used to increase revenue, cuts costs, or both.

Data-mining software is one of a number of tools for analysing data. It allows users to analyse data from many different dimensions or angles, categorise it, and summarise the relationships identified. In other words, data mining is finding patterns among dozens of fields in large relational databases.

Data, information and knowledge

Data are any facts and figures that can be processed by a computer. Today, organisations are accumulating vast and growing amounts of data in different formats and different databases. This includes:

- **operational or transactional data**, such as sales, cost, inventory, payroll and accounting;
- **non-operational data**, such as industry sales, forecast data and macroeconomic data;
- **meta data** – data about the data itself – such as logical database design or data dictionary definitions.

The patterns, associations, or relationships among all this data can provide information. For example, analysis of retail point-of-sale transaction data can yield information on which products are selling and when.

Information can be converted into knowledge about historical patterns and future trends. For example, summary information on retail supermarket sales can be analysed in the light of promotional efforts to provide knowledge of consumer buying behaviour. Thus a manufacturer or retailer could determine which items are most susceptible to promotional efforts.

An ever-increasing desire for better (or at least more) information and deeper (or at least more) knowledge has been accompanied by dramatic advances in data capture, processing power, data transmission and storage capabilities, which are enabling organisations to integrate their various databases into data warehouses and to maximise user access and analysis.

Mining for what?

Data mining is primarily used by companies with a strong consumer focus: retail, financial, communication and marketing. It enables them to determine relationships among "internal" factors such as price, product positioning or staff skills, and "external" factors such as economic indicators, competition and customer demographics. It also enables them to determine the impact on sales, customer satisfaction, and corporate profits. Lastly, it enables them to "drill down" into summary information to view detailed transactional data.

With data mining, a retailer could use point-of-sale records of customer purchases to send targeted promotions based on an individual's purchase history. By mining demographic data from customer feedback forms or warranty agreements, the retailer could develop products and promotions to appeal to specific customer segments.

For example, American Express can suggest products to its cardholders based on analysis of their monthly expenditure. Tesco's introduction of the Clubcard loyalty scheme in 1995 was widely seen as a masterstroke, enabling the retailer to analyse purchasing data to dovetail precisely individual customer preferences with special offers. Tesco has extended the scheme to 11 countries in which it operates and is considering how to adapt the scheme for its ailing American brand, Fresh & Easy.

B&Q, a British multinational DIY and home improvement retailer, announced in January 2011 that it would be using data mining to strengthen the link between customer "input" and business decisions. This input comes in the form of direct feedback from its "Voice" website, online discussion forums and chat rooms and purchasing data from its stores. B&Q is forming a joint venture with a London-based data consultancy to help it make maximum use of this information.

Walmart

Walmart is pioneering massive data mining to transform its supplier relationships. It captures point-of-sale transactions from over 2,900 stores in six countries and continuously transmits the data to its massive 7.5 terabyte data warehouse. Walmart allows more than 3,500 suppliers to access data on their products and perform data analyses. The suppliers use the data to identify customer buying patterns at the store display level, and then use this information to manage local store inventory and identify new merchandising opportunities.

Ian Cheshire, B&Q's CEO, commented:[6]

[This new joint venture] will really create a much, much sharper data-mining capability, and we'll have all the information coming together in one place, with a customer officer whose job is to make sure that we are absolutely listening to the customer ... Making that transition from being a seller of products to someone who can read what customers are doing is a big cultural shift.

Double-loop learning

Double-loop learning is not a new concept. Its originator, Chris Argyris, a Harvard Business School professor, first developed the idea over 30 years ago. But the onset of a more uncertain business environment has made it even more relevant to predictive learning at a time when organisations need to respond effectively to sudden opportunities or threats.

Double-loop learning is when an individual, organisation or entity is able, having attempted to achieve a goal on different occasions, to modify the goal in the light of experience or possibly even reject it. Single-loop learning is the repeated attempt at the same problem, with no variation of method and without ever questioning the goal.

This is how Argyris described the process in 1978:[7]

When an error detected and corrected permits the organisation to carry on its present policies or achieve its present objectives, then that error-and-correction process is single-loop learning. Single-loop learning is like a thermostat that learns when it is too hot or too cold and turns the heat on or off. The thermostat can perform this task because it can receive information (the temperature of the room) and take corrective action. Double-loop learning occurs when an error is detected and corrected in ways that involve the modification of an organisation's underlying norms, policies and objectives.

Single-loop learning seems to be present when goals, values, frameworks and, to a significant extent, strategies are taken for granted. The emphasis is on "techniques and making techniques more efficient". Any reflection is directed toward making the strategy more effective. Double-loop learning, in contrast, "involves questioning the role of the framing and learning systems which underlie actual goals and strategies".

As Argyris said later in 1982, in many respects the distinction at work here is the one used by Aristotle, when exploring technical and practical thought.[8] The former involves following routines and some sort of preset plan – which is less risky for the individual and the organisation and affords greater control. The latter is more creative and reflexive, and involves consideration about notions of the good. Reflection here is more fundamental, he wrote. "The basic assumptions behind ideas or policies are confronted ... hypotheses are publicly tested ... processes are disconfirmable, not self-seeking."

Among the senior executives interviewed as a follow-up to the managing uncertainty survey carried out for this book, double-loop learning took the form of attempting to capture and codify the experiences of employees of managing in a crisis or learning from mistakes.

As noted earlier, RBS, following its crash in 2009, used knowledge-management technology and tools developed in conjunction with Accenture to capture and codify the experiences of its surviving executives so that this experience could be learned from in the future. "We see our leaders as teachers," commented RBS's Donna Hamilton.

Many other executives interviewed said much the same.

Ceridian

We work through and learn from our staff the impact that they have on our customers when they do good things and they do bad things. It is not necessarily the decision-making that is devolved but the feedback we capture about the impact our people make on our customers.

All this is about adopting a clearer way of identifying and then recognising internally that "Fred over there" has had a massively positive impact on the company, and leveraging that experience and ability for the benefit of ten other Freds. Far too much essential knowledge lies dormant in the heads of our best people rather than being fed into our management and operational systems.

Nick Laird

Deutsche Bank

Deutsche Bank has set up a commitment index of staff attitudes, commitment and work experiences. Klaus Mittorp, former director, HR communications and quality (now senior vice-president at

Abduction

This kind of frontline feedback is crucial to what Henry Mintzberg, professor of management studies at McGill University, calls organisational "abduction". He describes abduction as "the burst of knowing that occurs when we listen and talk to each other".[9] It is the process by which people use their existing mental models to make sense of their experiences. In turn, new mental models are created. "Abduction," he says, "is the method of building strategy from the middle levels of the organisation."

Abduction, as an organisation process, is built around seven propositions:

Hay Group Germany), explained that anything that can provide an accurate "pulse-take" of the health of the organisation is critically important not only to HR's own performance but also to the bank's competitive standing. Pulse-taking could include capturing frontline best practice, or spotting early trends that will lead to declining performance in time for line managers to capture and use this feedback.

Mittorp elaborates:

The commitment index has enabled the bank to link its concept of engagement and commitment with its strategic goals. The ability of the index to provide senior managers and business unit managers with reports about employees' engagement with their work, their emotional link with the bank's core values and details of their frontline good practice has been pivotal to the bank's ability to manage operational risk. The commitment index is a particularly important plank in its philosophy of "strategic readiness" in the face of uncertain times.

1. Effective strategic decisions emerge from a communicative interaction among relevant organisational members.
2. Relevant organisational members include operational managers and frontline employees.
3. The role of middle management is to make sure that the ideas of operational-level employees are included.
4. Unexpected events are not to be ignored or eradicated, but used as opportunities for abduction among the levels of management.
5. Deviations from the expected are worthy of abductive understanding.

6. The role of top management is to be flexible in its interpretations and, though willing to navigate by strategic vision, be responsive to change.

7. Firms employing emergent strategies invite and support experimentation.

Critical to Mintzberg's concept of abduction is collective decision-making that spreads across the whole organisation. The importance of this was highlighted by executives interviewed for this book. As the learning and development manager of one of Europe's leading technology firms says:

Future expansion will require a different set of skills and a different way of managing and developing the business. We don't know how to do it. We don't know what the future skills set will be and this is a big problem. The future involves risk and a new definition of the business. We will need a strongly collaborative mindset across the business – no one operating company can do it alone, we need to be together. We are far away from this mindset.

Also implicit in the concept of abduction is senior decision-makers adopting an open mind and actively opening themselves up to new ideas. Again, one of the interviewees, Chris Stephenson, who has worked in organisations ranging from Egg, a British internet bank, to the UK Ministry of Justice, told us:

I would say that overall, organisations need to learn to acknowledge and talk about uncertainty. In today's world, it's impossible for managers to be aware of and conceivably understand every aspect of their environment.

It's my belief and experience that the bulk of managers, even senior managers, are not allowed to talk about uncertainty. There's the assumption that the whole purpose of management is to provide certainty. Senior managers do not spend enough time away from the business talking about uncertainty or what the future looks like.

Frankly, that is what the job of executives should be. They should be pushing out their thinking to five or ten years hence, and have the capability to ask the questions that need to be asked. There will be people out there with views about the future and they should be asking them the right questions and listening to them. That form of data gathering and processing by the executive team is a vital part of managing uncertainty.

Building a predictive learning culture

Predictive learning is a complex blend of technological expertise, new learning approaches and a willingness among a critical mass of employees to develop peripheral vision, where tiny shifts and dissonances in the external market are investigated. Equally important, companies need to act on this intelligence in a timely manner, which of course requires knowing when various subtle cues fit together to form enough information for the business to move.

Businesses will make mistakes as they try to anticipate market transitions and disruptions, but the only way to build capability in predictive learning is by being willing to take risks and act on incomplete and ambiguous intelligence. Firms can nurture predictive learning in several ways:

- Senior managers must champion the need for staff to probe the unknown and the uncertain.
- The business case for predictive learning must be explained to employees, showing where such learning has led to tangible benefits and providing clear strategic direction so that they focus on areas of uncertainty that could yield the biggest rewards or the highest value opportunities.
- Information and tacit knowledge must move across the organisation and not get trapped.
- Training and development must emphasise learning and give employees tools to reflect on their experiences, ask questions, share their perspectives with colleagues and contribute to any formal learning or knowledge-management processes.
- The culture must encourage debate and speculative and opportunistic learning, so staff are able to share ideas informally and have time and space to look beyond their day-to-day concerns and think about the future.

Adopting an integrated approach

Data mining, analytics and abduction are sequential processes. It is only through a combination of all three that organisations can achieve the kind of predictive learning described in this chapter. Two examples illustrate this combination in practice: Cisco Systems and IBM.

Cisco Systems

Cisco Systems has achieved predictive learning largely through the leadership of its chief executive, John Chambers, who joined the company in 1991 as senior vice-president, worldwide sales and operations. Since January 1995, when he assumed the role of CEO, Cisco's annual revenues have grown from $1.2 billion to approximately $40 billion. Before joining Cisco he spent eight years at Wang Laboratories and six at IBM.

During his time as CEO, Chambers has developed an uncanny ability to sense market trends long before others do. He predicted, for instance, that voice transmission would become free long before computer networks could even carry it; and Cisco was the first company to shift from call centres to web-based customer service.

Anticipating and responding to future market trends is essential for a company that must start developing a product up to six years before it goes to market. Chambers has succeeded in this task through a combination of the methods outlined in this chapter.

He looks for what he calls "market disruptions" – his term for hidden signals that encompass subtle social, economic or technological signs of impending trends that "predictive" organisations can pick up 5–7 years before the rest of the market grasps their significance.[10] The move to open-source software development, for example, was one that Cisco predicted and acted on and Microsoft did not.

Chambers senses these trends, and has done for decades, by listening closely to customers and "connecting individual dots of behaviour into patterns that indicate these trends". He drew on his own sensing skills to upend Cisco's management processes, surrendering his role as a "command and control" CEO and instituting collaborative decision-making that allows the company to respond rapidly to emerging trends (although he has been hotly criticised for this change and dismantled some of this structure in 2011 – see Chapter 4).

Managers at Cisco now form cross-functional teams working together to identify and exploit new opportunities quickly, allowing Cisco to implement simultaneously 22 major sales initiatives as quickly as most other companies do one or two.

IBM

IBM has developed a culture of "corporate foresight", which it defines as the structured capability of an enterprise to sense, explore and prepare for how the future may emerge and to use that insight in formulating strategy, plans and operations.

Sam Palmisano, IBM's chairman, argues that the company's capacity to adopt a longer perspective of its market and the corporate environment in which it operates is a major asset and a competitive advantage. It:[11]

- determines how and where you invest and allocate resources;
- changes your view of talent development;
- guides the ethics and behaviour of both management and employees;
- shapes the way you see your company's role in industry and in society;
- tells you how and when to take decisive action.

Today, IBM has a diverse, evolving set of internal foresight centres focused on technology, society and business, each of which involves different stakeholders, structures, purposes, locations within the business and timeframes. Together they form a comprehensive system of looking towards the future that IBM can act upon. These centres include:

- **Global Technology Outlook (GTO).** For more than 25 years, IBM Research has prepared an annual study of major technology trends for the company's senior management team. The GTO analysis looks at the innovations that may have a significant impact on businesses worldwide, especially those in the IT industry. The GTO helps drive IBM's $6 billion investment in research and development each year.

- **Academy of Technology (AoT).** The AoT focuses on the technical underpinnings of IBM's future. The elected membership comprises the technical leaders from IBM locations around the world. Member-initiated activities include independent consultancies for executives, studies and workshops, and topical conferences.

- **Global Innovation Outlook (GIO).** Annually since 2004, IBM has brought together people from all over the world to discuss their ideas about the major issues on the horizon in a variety of areas, such as natural resources, security and emerging markets. The GIO takes a deep look at some of the most pressing issues facing the world and shares insights on providing solutions to those needs.

- **IBM Institute for Business Value (IBV).** A global team of more than 50 IBV consultants conducts research and analysis across multiple industries and functional disciplines. The IBV also produces thought-leadership papers, for example industry views on the future of market segments such as retail and health care.

- **InnovationJam.** InnovationJams are online forum discussions that typically run over a period of 1–3 days. They are tightly managed and enable senior executives to engage with participants on two or three questions or challenges. An InnovationJam in 2006 played a crucial role in IBM's "Smarter Planet" initiative.

- **Market Development and Insights.** IBM's internal market-research organisation explores and analyses potential future landscapes, assists decision-makers in developing and exploiting new market opportunities, and helps to identify future sources of value. Analysts use sophisticated techniques to develop a global perspective on high-potential industries, emerging technologies, competition and new markets. IBM is also one of the few corporations to conduct futures research (see Chapter 2).

In November 2008, in a speech at the Council on Foreign Relations, Palmisano outlined a new agenda for building a "Smarter Planet". He said that the world's systems and industries are becoming more instrumented (that is, engineered), interconnected and intelligent, and that leaders and citizens can take advantage of this to improve these systems and industries.[12]

Smarter Planet as an exercise in foresight began with one of the IBM processes outlined above. In 2006, a global InnovationJam brought together more than 150,000 people in 100 countries – IBM employees, their families, clients and others – in a virtual brainstorming session on emerging business opportunities. Several concepts developed during that session were the beginnings of technologies that today are helping the world become a smarter place.

Since introducing the Smarter Planet concept, IBM has collaborated with more than 600 organisations worldwide so that each plays its part in making this vision a reality.

8   Conclusion: creating an integrated approach

Managing uncertainty is integral to my work. If there is one thing you can be absolutely certain about, it is that the world is uncertain. That has to be the starting point for managing any form of activity or transaction. If you are not sufficiently clear that you are working in the context of an uncertain world, your plans will fail.

Chris Stephenson, States of Jersey

THIS CHAPTER DRAWS TOGETHER the main lessons in this book about how to manage uncertainty better. The global financial crisis provided a rare opportunity to analyse how companies responded to an unprecedented degree of turbulence, what they have learned from the experience and how it had changed their attitude to management.

The managing uncertainty survey carried out for this book and the follow-up interviews brought out the following:

■ **Firms were being buffeted not by just one but several sources of uncertainty.** In the survey, it was clear that in the fallout from the financial crisis respondents were extremely concerned about the scale of uncertainty and the range of different uncertainties affecting their businesses.

■ **Uncertainty is a new business reality that has to be managed.** Over 70% of those surveyed said that the crisis had made them realise they should put more consideration into how to manage uncertainty and risk within their business. But they viewed managing uncertainty as distinct from enterprise risk management and other related management disciplines, such as crisis management or change management.

■ **There is no single strategy for managing uncertainty.** Every company must hone a strategy that is best adapted to their environment and competitive situation and executed using their unique blend of skills and resources. Traditional approaches to strategy determination and execution as well as risk and change management needed to be adapted for conditions that were volatile and complex, interrelated and highly unpredictable.

■ **The need for senior managers to accept that managing uncertainty is a crucial part of their role and responsibility.** As one interviewee said: "There is nothing in my job title but it [managing uncertainty] is a phrase that resonates with me. It a phrase we use a lot in the organisation. We use it both in the sense of an individual's ability to manage ambiguity and in the sense that the organisation is dealing with a rapidly changing world and market and is trying to work out the right way to go about it."

■ **Uncertainty can be the "elephant" in the executive suite.** Although interviewees attached the greatest importance to anticipating and responding effectively to uncertainty, paradoxically many admitted that among their executive teams there was a reluctance to discuss uncertainty openly and that the wider organisation was not encouraged to.

Many firms are moving into unfamiliar terrain as they learn to manage uncertainty. Those taking their first steps need to take on board the following:

■ Accept the reality of increased uncertainty. The current economic turbulence will subside in time but there will be other uncertainties to deal with.

■ Senior managers must talk openly about the uncertainty and potential volatility and turbulence their business faces to investors and analysts and other stakeholders, most importantly their employees. They need to display confidence about the unknown and the unpredictable and to be ready to revise their plans and strategies when changing circumstances demand.

■ Managing uncertainty needs to be recognised as a crucial leadership and management skill. There must be a learning and development strategy in place to prepare tomorrow's business leaders (and indeed leaders in general) to work comfortably in highly fluid, complex business environments.

Reconfiguring businesses to manage uncertainty

Many organisations are rethinking some of their fundamental assumptions about how to do business in a highly uncertain and competitive global environment. Senior executives identified a number of transitions as essential to managing uncertainty effectively. These can be clustered under the following headings.

Strategic planning

■ From management by objectives to scenario and contingency planning.

■ From "seeing it as you wish it" to "seeing it as it is".

■ From five-year strategic cycles to "three-year strategy broken down into one-year cycles".

■ From "strategic planning looking at the past" to "an empirical methodology to come up with possible outcomes in the future".

■ From fear of the future to "finding it attractive that the future is unwritten and that we are well-positioned to do well because of the diversity and adaptability of our business".

■ From "seeing the future through the business" to "seeing the future through the broader world".

■ From "working with perfect information" to "a willingness and ability to cope with diverging bits of information and opinion".

■ From traditional strategic planning based on quarterly trends to "achieving a balance between the delivery of strategy and the determination of strategy – and thus shortening the process".

Risk management

- From risk management focused on managing the downside to "managing the upside as well as the downside, placing bets on things that may have a low probability of success but a high upside".

- From risk management "as a precursor to managing uncertainty" to "risk management as an outcome of managing uncertainty".

- From risk management as a procedure to "managing uncertainty as an ongoing process".

- From risk management as an analytical process to "managing uncertainty as something intuitive".

- From "crisis as a threat" to "crisis as an opportunity".

Leadership

- From a communication strategy based on "saying nothing, leaving people to feel less certain of themselves and less likely to take action" to "turning up the volume, creating confidence and a positivity that pervades the organisation".

- From top-down leadership to "walking the talk, ensuring employees buy into what actions we are taking and taking part in developing the right solutions".

- From top-down leadership to "providing some level of comfort and leadership and direction even when you are not sure what that direction is going to be in a year's time" (for example, pursuing a commitment to globalisation even when it is unclear which countries or regions will be given priority because of uncertain shifts in exchange rates).

- From "decisions thought out to the nth degree" to "squaring with the workforce, not infantilising them" (that is, being honest with the workforce, not patronising them).

- From decision-making based on a purely internal perspective to "adopting an external perspective, building resilient leaders means building people who are comfortable with ambiguity, uncertainty and managing paradox – to do that they need excellent external sensing skills."

■ From a homogeneous leadership and mindset to "a diverse and collaborative mindset across the business".

■ From imposing good practice from above to "releasing and capturing good practice from our staff".

■ From a "formulaic, numbers-driven, deliberative planning process" to "painting a vivid picture of the future that people can latch onto – but bearing in mind at the same time that this picture might change".

Operational management

■ From centralised decision-making to "a collegiate and collaborative approach to making strategic decisions".

■ From target-based management to "giving people time to reflect, talk to people, share creative ideas and talk about our customers and how their requirements are changing".

■ From "seeing knowledge as personal power" to "sharing best practice, getting people to network".

■ From R&D to "getting every employee at every level of the business talking to clients and understanding their views".

■ From cutting overheads to reduce costs to "cutting overheads to create the foundation for future growth".

■ From centralised decision-making to "getting people to make decisions and lead in their own market".

Stakeholder management

■ From narrowly based shareholder management to holistic stakeholder management.

■ From "strategy resulting from internalised dialogue" to "breaking down the walls of the organisation and connecting with the external world".

■ From internal R&D to "working with cross-industry bodies to create and share common technologies and solutions".

■ From proprietorial technology to "sharing resources and facilities with non-competing firms in the same industry".

Talent management

■ From traditional succession planning to "looking at the changing skills that will be required in the organisation in the future and that will lead us to the best place in the industry to capitalise on opportunities as they arise – something we can absolutely control".

Developing a capabilities framework

These findings confirmed that companies are rethinking their shape and purpose as they move into an increasingly complex, unpredictable world. Managing uncertainty may well be the biggest challenge facing today's generation of business leaders and, in the face of continuing uncertainty, capability in this area will become ever more important.

However, this first phase of the research threw up a major challenge: how could uncertainty be explored when every company was facing its own unique mix of uncertainties? Each business's experience of uncertainty is different, but two axes, level of ambiguity and pace of change, are a crude but effective way of describing levels of uncertainty.

Interviewees were asked what would help them manage uncertainty effectively. In response, there was a plea for case studies and practical examples of how organisations were attempting to manage uncertainty – successfully or otherwise – and for a framework that would help "scope" an otherwise nebulous concept into a set of questions or priorities that leaders could explore. One interviewee said:

> I need a template to help me address questions. The whole thing about this issue is that it is so broad, so interesting and so uncertain that you end up either sitting there and not doing anything because you are so paralysed by the scale of it, or are focusing on a little area and getting lost.

Another important issue was organisational capabilities, as the following comment illustrates:

TABLE 8.1 **Strategic readiness: six capabilities**

Strategic anticipation	The capability to determine and the ability to implement a strategy that is highly responsive to an unpredictable and potentially volatile environment
Navigational leadership	The capability to instil a collective sense of where the organisation is and the confidence and optimism to move forward into an uncertain future
Agility	The capability to move rapidly and flexibly in order to shape or adapt to the threats and opportunities arising from uncertainty
Resilience	The capability to absorb and positively build on adversity, shocks and setbacks
Open collaboration	The capability to dissolve boundaries, forge links and reach outside through partnerships and the sharing of ideas and information to gain a broader perspective and maximise innovation
Predictive learning	The capability to sense, probe and analyse previously hidden patterns and trends in order to anticipate sudden or disruptive change

Source: © Michel Syrett and Marion Devine, 2012

I would like to gain more insight about how to create a more flexible and agile organisation so that it can respond quickly to changes in the environment – by introducing new processes or developing new capabilities that the organisation needs to achieve this goal.

It is plain that there is no single strategy for managing uncertainty. Each organisation must hone a strategy that is best adapted to its particular circumstances, skills and resources.

However, a set of common themes and priorities emerged from the interviews and survey findings. Although many organisations are struggling to manage uncertainty, leaders have a strong sense of some of the actions and attitudes that help them deal with uncertain or chaotic contexts. From these it is possible to identify a set of capabilities, which together create a state of "strategic readiness", where a business is prepared and equipped to respond positively to prolonged uncertainty and sudden, unpredictable shifts in the external environment (see Table 8.1).

These six capabilities are tightly interlinked and so organisations need to build expertise in all of them. For example, in uncertain environments, an organisation needs to be able to sense and probe, but open collaboration helps maximise its opportunities to draw in many different sources of information. Predictive learning and open collaboration help alert an organisation to threats and opportunities from uncertainty and thus feed into the capacity for strategic anticipation. Learning and collaboration at all levels help employees and leaders to be more aware of, and thus more resilient to, the stresses and strains of an unpredictable environment. Strong navigational leadership also helps build resilience, which then helps generate the energy and commitment necessary for agile changes of direction.

Plotting a pathway

Contrary to the views of management thinkers like Gary Hamel and Charles Handy, it can be argued that, in times of uncertainty, changes in approach to management are evolutionary, not revolutionary. They shift according to circumstances.

In the case of the approaches highlighted in Chapters 2–7, the circumstances are determined by the interplay of two polarities affecting the business environment in which organisations operate:

- pace of change;
- level of ambiguity.

These are crude but useful indicators for helping firms assess the degree of uncertainty within a specific business context or environment. Senior managers can then judge whether their management processes are fit for purpose in an environment that could range from predictable and slowly changing through to highly uncertain. Figures 8.1–3 look at the impact of uncertainty on three aspects of managing uncertainty: strategy, leadership and organisational response.

Strategy

The four quadrants in Figure 8.1 can be described as follows.

Low pace of change, low level of ambiguity
This is a clear enough future, consisting of a single forecast precise enough for determining strategy. In these circumstances, the

FIG 8.1 **The impact of uncertainty on strategy**

		LEVEL OF AMBIGUITY	
		Low	High
PACE OF CHANGE	High	Option evaluation Game theory Decision analysis	Pattern recognition/analogy
	Low	Traditional business planning	Technology forecasting Scenario planning

Source: © Michel Syrett and Marion Devine, 2012

traditional approach of setting out a forecast of the future precise enough to be captured in traditional business-planning systems such as a discounted cash-flow analysis will work effectively.

High pace of change, low level of ambiguity
These are alternate futures, consisting of a few discrete outcomes that define the future. In these circumstances, decision analysis, option valuation and game theory can be used to inform the right decisions.

Low pace of change, high level of ambiguity
This is a range of futures, consisting of a range of possible outcomes, but no natural scenarios. In these circumstances, technology forecasting and scenario planning can be used to inform the right decisions.

High pace of change, high level of ambiguity
This is true ambiguity, where there is no basis to forecast the future. In these circumstances, strategists need to fall back on analogies and pattern recognition.

See Chapter 2 for a more detailed explanation of each of these techniques and responses.

Leadership

The four quadrants in Figure 8.2 can be described as follows.

Low pace of change, low level of ambiguity

In this scenario, where there is an emphasis on maintaining and exploiting quality and excellence in a status quo, the priority for senior managers is to ensure that the implementation of strategy is not impeded by "friction" such as turf wars, poor allocation of resources, and poor interpretation at middle and lower management levels. The basic message is as true today as it ever was: that successful strategy execution is about clarity of purpose, good communication, strictly controlled resource allocation, breaking strategy down into easily achieved objectives and fostering a risk-friendly culture that encourages freedom of action if it supports strategic goals. See *Successful Strategy Execution* by Michel Syrett.[1]

High pace of change, low level of ambiguity

In this scenario, the role of visionary leadership – as pioneered in the 1980s by GE's Jack Welch, Virgin's Richard Branson and The Body Shop's Anita Roddick – is paramount. As described by Charles Handy, a management thinker, the vision in a time of fast change but with a clear outlook of the future must be different.[2] It must be understood by the whole workforce and, as Handy puts it, "the leader must live the vision" in a way that requires significant self-belief.

Low pace of change, high level of ambiguity

In this scenario, leadership means not communicating a single vision and clear direction for the organisation, but rather creating and communicating options. As articulated by Hugh Courtney, Jane Kirkland and Patrick Viguerie, organisations reserve the right to play, investing sufficiently to "stay in the game" but avoiding premature commitments.[3] This involves making incremental investments today that put an organisation in a privileged position, either through superior information and cost structures or through relationships between customers and suppliers. This allows an organisation to wait until the environment becomes less uncertain before formulating a strategy.

FIG 8.2 **The impact of uncertainty on leadership**

		LEVEL OF AMBIGUITY	
		Low	High
PACE OF CHANGE	High	Creating and communicating a clear direction	Creating and communicating confidence and context
	Low	Traditional execution strategy	Creating and communicating options

Source: © Michel Syrett and Marion Devine, 2012

High pace of change, high level of ambiguity

In this scenario, as Chapter 3 explores, leadership means communicating and instilling confidence in the organisation's ability to anticipate and respond to unexpected threats and opportunities that might occur in an uncertain environment. It also means creating and communicating a context that, as one of the executives interviewed put it, makes people believe "they can make a difference, that they can help build a positive picture of the future".

Organisational response

The four quadrants in Figure 8.3 can be described as follows.

Low pace of change, low level of ambiguity

In this scenario, where strategy execution is at a premium, the model of organisational response championed by the total quality management (TQM) ethic of the 1980s is still valid. The priority should be effective communication of strategic goals, coupled with measures to ensure that these goals are understood clearly and "owned" by the workforce. Kathleen McKone, a professor at Babson College, and her colleague, Roger Schroeder, have identified the nine

FIG 8.3 **The organisational response to uncertainty**

		LEVEL OF AMBIGUITY	
		Low	High
PACE OF CHANGE	High	Change management	Agility and predictive learning
	Low	Traditional quality management	Partnership and collaboration

Source: © Michel Syrett and Marion Devine, 2012

common TQM practices as cross-functional product design, process management, supplier quality management, customer involvement, information and feedback, committed leadership, strategic planning, cross-functional training, and employee involvement.[4]

High pace of change, low level of ambiguity
In this scenario, where creating and communicating a clear direction or vision of the future is at a premium, conventional change management is still valid. This is a structured approach to shifting/ transitioning individuals, teams and the organisation from a current state to a desired future state and helping employees to accept and embrace changes in their current business environment. This will involve creating a business case for the change (which should be continuously updated) and effective communication of the reasons for the change that informs and inspires all stakeholders. Traditional change management also includes devising effective training and development for upgrading the organisation, countering any resistance from employees and aligning them to the overall direction of the organisation.

Low pace of change, high level of uncertainty

In this scenario, achieving the organisational capability of open collaboration, as described in Chapter 6, is a priority. Through collaboration, a firm can reach beyond its boundaries, both mental and organisational, and link with others to understand and anticipate sources of uncertainty and their potential impact. Collaboration becomes a powerful means of adapting to an uncertain environment. Through linking up with external organisations and customers, as well as encouraging internal collaborative working, an organisation can try to resolve confusion, uncertainty and mixed signals from the environment. This can help an organisation absorb new ideas and perspectives from a diverse array of collaborative partners, enhancing its ability to spot sudden shifts in customer or competitive behaviour or the emergence of disruptive technology. Ultimately, the ability to collaborate will help an organisation to keep learning and innovating.

High pace of change, high level of uncertainty

In this scenario, achieving the twin organisational capabilities of agility and predictive learning is the priority. As highlighted in Chapter 4, many of the companies that took part in the managing uncertainty survey and the follow-up interviews are debating how they can become more agile by responding quickly and flexibly to uncertain conditions or shaping events to their own advantage – and they are achieving this through a combination of financial agility, operational agility, portfolio agility and organisational agility.

Similarly, Chapter 2 argues that the quality of an organisation's strategy depends on the quality of the knowledge it draws on. This in turn hinges on how effectively the process of knowledge gaining is managed in the organisation. Strategy formulation must therefore be regarded as a constant learning process, and the quality of strategy depends on the quality of the organisation's cognitive and behavioural learning mechanisms. Chapter 7 stressed the effective use of data mining, pattern recognition, strategic analysis and double-loop learning – in which an individual, organisation or entity is able, having attempted to achieve a goal on different occasions, to modify that goal in the light of experience or possibly even reject it.

Conclusion

The goal of this book is to offer a systematic way for organisations to navigate a way through periods of prolonged uncertainty. Exploring the uncertainties of the current and future business environment is critical for long-term commercial success, and managing uncertainty should be a high priority for senior management. Employees also have a responsibility to engage with uncertainty. They should expect clarity and focus about their organisation's strategic direction, but they cannot expect to be shielded from the reality of an uncertain world.

By making uncertainty a topic of debate, senior management can help focus their organisations on the unique "context" in which they operate and the range of "known unknowns" and "unknown unknowns" that might exist and potentially lead to new competitive opportunities.

The capabilities framework, which constitutes strategic readiness, is not a prescriptive model. It is simply a starting point to help an organisation assess whether its business is correctly aligned to its external environment. Is some or the whole of the organisation focused on certainty to the point of myopia? If the balance were to be shifted towards more uncertainty, would this reveal the need to build capability in some or all areas of strategic readiness? By looking at the business through the lens of strategic readiness, where are these capabilities already evident and how might they be shared across the business in a process that will help embed them deeper into operational and cultural processes throughout the organisation?

The final message is that uncertainty creates both opportunities and risk. Organisations that seek to ignore it are in danger of being buffeted by unforeseen and potentially destructive forces. Uncertainty will build to the point where an organisation finds itself wholly out of kilter with its environment – forcing it to embark on crisis management and business turnaround. The alternative is to engage with uncertainty and have the confidence and vision to seize the initiative and turn uncertainty into opportunity. The organisations that learn to manage uncertainty will be those that thrive in the coming decades.

Appendix **Managing uncertainty survey**

PA Consulting Group (PA), in collaboration with the authors, conducted a survey of 205 senior executives from international companies and public-sector organisations in various countries and regions in spring 2011. In analysing the data, survey responses were compared with total shareholder return (TSR) for the organisations involved (92 in total).

In a follow-up to the survey the authors interviewed 13 of the 205 respondents. Those who kindly agreed to give up their time to be interviewed are listed below:

Letizia Amadini-Lane, head of R&D leadership culture
GlaxoSmithKline (UK-based pharmaceutical company)

Dan Flint, HR director
Simmons & Simmons (UK-based international law firm)

Daniel Galvao, chief commercial officer and senior vice-president
Marsh (US-based insurance broker and risk adviser)

Richard Gartside, director, talent and leadership development
Balfour Beatty (UK-based construction and engineering company)

Donna Hamilton, head of group learning
RBS (Royal Bank of Scotland)

Ian Howells, general manager
Honda Europe (part of the Japan-based automobile manufacturer)

Nick Laird, chief commercial officer
Ceridian (US-based human resources and payroll outsourcing
    company)

Neil Morrison, group HR director
Random House (US-based publishing company)

Praful Pillay, senior vice-president
SunGard India (part of US-based SunGard Technology Services,
    business services outsourcing firm)

Shivakumar Rajagopalin, former chief financial officer
Wipro Infocrossing (part of India-based Wipro, IT outsourcing firm)

Adrian Rawcliffe, senior vice-president, worldwide business
    development for R&D
GlaxoSmithKline (UK-based pharmaceutical company)

Neil Schloss, vice-president and treasurer
Ford Motor Company (US-based automobile manufacturer)

Chris Stephenson, director, operations and HR transformation
States of Jersey (government of Jersey)

Iain Worsley, senior vice-president (finance)
Capital One Bank (US-based retail bank)

Questionnaire

The interviews with the senior managers listed above were based on
their responses to the questionnaire, which is in two sections. The first
section deals with events during the financial crisis from 2007 when
Northern Rock hit the headlines through to the bail-out of Irish banks
in late 2010. The second section explores how respondents' attitudes
towards managing other uncertainties and risks have changed since.

Please answer questions by circling around the number which best :

Questions		Strongly agree				Strongly disagree
A.1	Before the financial crisis, we had a well developed approach to managing uncertainty and planning strategies to deal with the unexpected within our business	1 2	3	4	5	
A.2	Our management board became aware that the financial crisis would have an impact on our business using scale between 1 to 9 to align with dates on the timeline above	1 2 3 4 5 6 7 8 9				
A.3	Of the below sources of information, insight and approaches, which **three** did you use the most to explore the impact the financial crisis would have on your business?					

Please rank your top three most extensively used methods, with 1 as the most extensively used method and the next two methods in descending order of importance as 2 and 3 respectively:

Source	Rank
Cross-industry bodies and governmental organisations	
Industry peers	
Briefings from independent experts	
Media	
Internal meetings with management and employees	
Strategic partners and suppliers	
Direct contact with strategically important customers	
Market research and focus groups to understand customer needs, attitudes and behaviours	
Market and customer analytics and numerical modelling	
Customer segmentation	
Scenario planning	
Desk research	
Other (please specify)	

Please state the extent to which you agree or disagree with the following statements:

	Questions	Strongly agree				Strongly disagree
A.4	Our company viewed the financial crisis primarily as an opportunity to advance rather than a threat to our business	1	2	3	4	5
A.5	We found it easy to find and collate all of the information we needed to enable evidence based decisions	1	2	3	4	5
A.6	Our dominant response to the crisis was geared towards preservation of profit rather than strengthening of long term competitive advantage	1	2	3	4	5
A.7	We believe our company made necessary decisions quickly and ahead of events unfolding rather than slowly so that events overtook us	1	2	3	4	5

A.8 Of the management groups below, which **three** played the largest roles in deciding your response to the financial crisis?

Please rank the top three groups that played the largest role in decision making, with 1 as the group that played the largest role, then the next two groups in decreasing order of input as 2 and 3 respectively:

Groups	Rank
1 or 2 very senior managers (and agreed by Board)	
Executive committee	
Business Unit heads	
Middle management	
Staff	
Strategic partners and suppliers	
Other (please specify)	

A.9 When did your business make its main decisions on how to respond to the financial crisis? Using a scale between 1 to 9 to align with dates on the timeline at the top of page 2

    1 2 3 4 5 6 7 8 9

Of the actions listed below, did your business respond to the financial crisis by:

	Questions	Yes, a significant activity				No, not at all
	Strategy					
A.10	Increasing the flexibility of strategic planning	1	2	3	4	5
A.11	Selling businesses and/or assets	1	2	3	4	5
A.12	Buying new businesses	1	2	3	4	5
A.13	Focusing on the profitable core	1	2	3	4	5
A.14	Investing in growth	1	2	3	4	5
	Market					
A.15	Forging stronger, closer relationships with key customers	1	2	3	4	5
A.16	Developing and redesigning innovative products, and technological development	1	2	3	4	5
A.17	Targeting new markets and customers	1	2	3	4	5
	Operations					
A.18	Improving operational efficiencies	1	2	3	4	5
A.19	Cutting costs	1	2	3	4	5
A.20	Reducing staff costs	1	2	3	4	5
	People					
A.21	Building capability, recruiting and developing talent	1	2	3	4	5
A.22	Empowering, enabling and mobilising staff	1	2	3	4	5
A.23	Instilling strong leadership and governance	1	2	3	4	5
A.24	Helping managers to take decisions despite incomplete, confusing or contradictory data	1	2	3	4	5

Please state the extent to which you agree or disagree with the following statements:

	Questions	Strongly agree				Strongly disagree
A.25	We are confident that we made the right decisions and improved how our business operates	1	2	3	4	5
A.26	We were both aware of and responded effectively to the actions of our competitors	1	2	3	4	5

Part B – Managing Uncertainty

Thinking about changes that may arise over the next three years, please rate the level of uncertainty and the potential impact on your business of changes in each of the areas below:

Questions	High uncertainty				Low uncertainty	High impact				Low impact
B.1 **Political** e.g. government austerity measures	1	2	3	4	5	1	2	3	4	5
B.2 **Economic** e.g. sovereign default	1	2	3	4	5	1	2	3	4	5
B.3 **Social** e.g. unemployment	1	2	3	4	5	1	2	3	4	5
B.4 **Technological** e.g. social media	1	2	3	4	5	1	2	3	4	5
B.5 **Legal** e.g. new regulation	1	2	3	4	5	1	2	3	4	5
B.6 **Environmental** e.g. emissions penalties	1	2	3	4	5	1	2	3	4	5
B.7 **Other** Please specify 1 _____	1	2	3	4	5	1	2	3	4	5
2 _____	1	2	3	4	5	1	2	3	4	5

B.8 After the financial crisis, we now put more consideration into how to actively manage uncertainty and risk within our business 1 2 3 4 5

B.9 Of the management groups below, which three now play the largest roles in deciding your response to future uncertainty?

Please rank the top **three** groups that play the largest role in decision making, with 1 as the group that play the largest role, then the next two groups in decreasing order of input as 2 and 3 respectively:

Groups	Rank
1 or 2 very senior managers (and agreed by Board)	
Executive committee	
Business Unit heads	
Middle management	
Staff	
Strategic partners and suppliers	
Other (please specify)	

Having learnt from the financial crisis, in future will your business respond to uncertainty by:

Questions		Yes, a significant activity				No, not at all
	Strategy					
B.10	Increasing the flexibility of strategic planning	1	2	3	4	5
B.11	Selling businesses and/or assets	1	2	3	4	5
B.12	Buying new businesses	1	2	3	4	5
B.13	Focusing on the profitable core	1	2	3	4	5
B.14	Investing in growth	1	2	3	4	5
	Market					
B.15	Forging stronger, closer relationships with key customers	1	2	3	4	5
B.16	Developing and redesigning innovative products, and technological development	1	2	3	4	5
B.17	Targeting new markets and customers	1	2	3	4	5
	Operations					
B.18	Improving operational efficiencies	1	2	3	4	5
B.19	Cutting costs	1	2	3	4	5
B.20	Reducing staff costs	1	2	3	4	5
	People					
B.21	Building capability, recruiting and developing talent	1	2	3	4	5
B.22	Empowering, enabling and mobilising staff	1	2	3	4	5
B.23	Instilling strong leadership and governance	1	2	3	4	5
B.24	Helping managers to take decisions despite incomplete, confusing or contradictory data	1	2	3	4	5

Selected survey results

The numbers in the chart titles relate to the questions in the questionnaire.

Part A –The financial crisis

A.I **Timescale: awareness that the financial crisis would have an impact on the business**

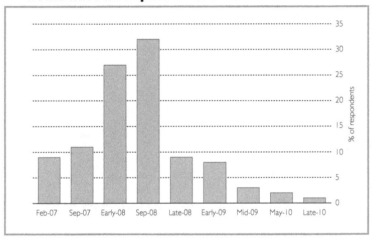

Source: © PA Knowledge 2011

A.2–6 **Approach to the crisis**

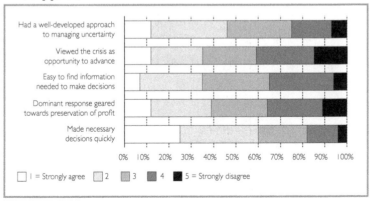

Source: © PA Knowledge 2011

A.7 **Groups with the largest roles in deciding response to the crisis**

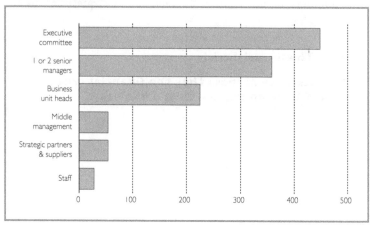

Source: © PA Knowledge 2011

A.8 **Sources most used to explore the impact of the crisis**

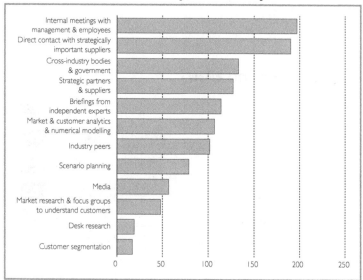

Source: © PA Knowledge 2011

A.9 **Timescale: when made main decisions on how to respond**

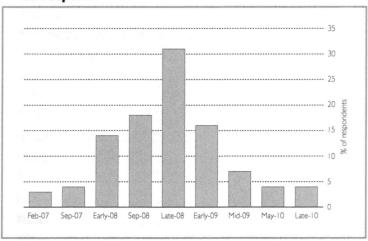

Source: © PA Knowledge 2011

A.10–24 **Responses to the crisis**

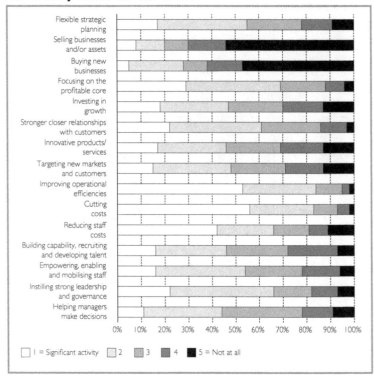

A.25 **Decision-making and competitor awareness**

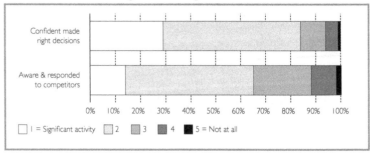

Part B – Managing uncertainty

B.1–7 **Areas of uncertainty**

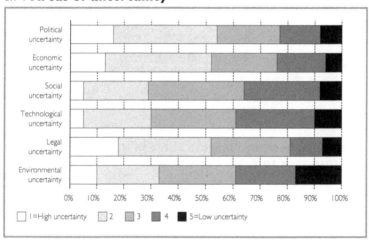

Source: © PA Knowledge 2011

B.1–7 **Areas of impact**

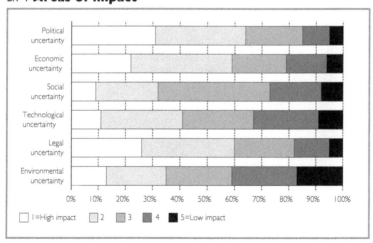

Source: © PA Knowledge 2011

B.15 **More consideration into managing uncertainty**

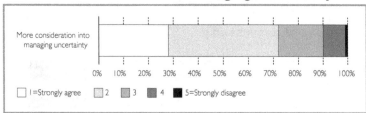

Source: © PA Knowledge 2011

B.16 **Groups with the largest roles in deciding response to future uncertainty**

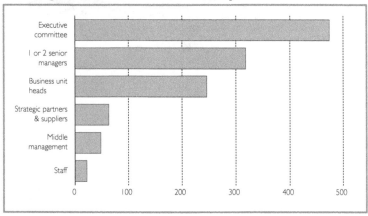

Source: © PA Knowledge 2011

B.17–31 **Future responses to uncertainty**

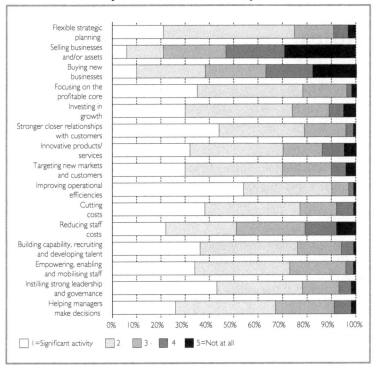

Source: © PA Knowledge 2011

Notes

1 Introduction: managing in an uncertain world

1 Power, K. and Day, A., *In the Thick of It: How are leaders and their organisations experiencing the economic crisis?*, Ashridge, February 2009.
2 Heifetz, R. *et al.*, "Leadership in a (Permanent) Crisis", *Harvard Business Review*, July 2009.
3 Nanto, D.K., *The Global Financial Crisis: Analysis and Policy Implications*, Congressional Research Service, October 2009.
4 Ibid.
5 *Dimensions of Uncertainty*, Foresight, UK Government Office for Science, 2010.
6 *Scenarios for the Future of Technology and International Development*, Rockefeller Foundation and Global Business Network, May 2010.
7 *Signals and Signposts: Shell Energy Scenarios to 2050*, Shell International BV, 2011.
8 De Meyer, A., "Managing Project Uncertainty: From Variation to Chaos", *MIT Sloan Management Review*, January 2002.

2 Strategic anticipation

1 Courtney, H., Kirkland, J. and Viguerie, P., "Strategy Under Uncertainty", *Harvard Business Review*, November–December 1997.
2 Ibid.
3 Brandenburger, A.M. and Nalebuff, B.J., *Co-opetition*, Currency Doubleday, 1996.
4 *Signals and Signposts: Shell Energy Scenarios to 2050*, Shell International BV, 2011.
5 Marakon, M.K. *et al.*, "Turning Strategy into Great Performance", *Harvard Business Review*, July 2005.
6 Feurer, R. and Chaharbaghi, K., "Strategy Development: Past, Present and Future", *Training for Quality*, Vol. 5, Issue 2, 1997.

7   Noronha, C., "Competing globally? It's a work in progress", *Tata Group Media Room*, May 2008.
8   Brown, B. and Scott, A., "How P&G Tripled its Innovation Success Rate", *Harvard Business Review*, June 2011.

3   Navigational leadership

1   Power, K. and Day, A., *In the Thick of It: How are leaders and their organisations experiencing the economic crisis?*, Ashridge, February 2009.
2   Hardman, P. and Nichols, C., "Stepping Lightly into Strategic Collaboration", *Converse*, Ashridge, Issue 6, 2009.
3   Syrett, M., *Successful Strategy Execution: How to keep your business goals on target*, Economist Books, hardback 2007, paperback 2011.
4   McKenzie, J. et al., "Cognition in Strategic Decision Making: a model of non-conventional thinking capacities for complex situations", *Management Decisions Journal*, Vol. 47, No. 2, 2009.
5   Ibid.

4   Agility

1   Elop, S., Nokia internal memo, leaked on February 11th 2011.
2   Sull, D., "Competing through Organisational Agility", *McKinsey Quarterly*, No. 1, 2010.
3   "Building a Nimble Organisation: a McKinsey Global Survey", *McKinsey Quarterly*, July 2006.
4   Glenn, M., *Organisational Agility: How Business can Survive and Thrive Through Turbulent Times*, Economist Intelligence Unit, 2009.
5   Voss, C. and Wang, C., *Agility in Services: Capabilities for Difficult Times*, London Business School, Advanced Institute of Management Research and the Institute of Customer Service, 2009.
6   Kaiser, K. and Young, D., "Blue Line Management: What Value Creation Really Means", *INSEAD Working Paper*, No. 2009/37/FIN/AC, July 2009. Available at SSRN: http://ssrn.com/abstract=1428388 or http://dx.doi.org/10.2139/ssrn.1428388
7   Ibid.
8   Bloch, M. and Lempres, E., "From Internal Services to Strategic Partner: an Interview with Filippo Passerini, President of P&G's Global Business Services", *McKinsey Quarterly*, July 2008.
9   "Toyota Gas Pedals: is the Public at Risk?", US Congressional Hearing, before the Committee on Oversight and Government Reform, US House of Representatives, 111 Congress, Second Session, Serial Number 111–75, February 24th 2010. Available from the US Government Printing Office (GPO) and at: http://frwebgate.access.gpo.gov/cgibin/getdoc.cgi?dbname=111_house_hearings&docid=f:58346.wais

10 Brown, S. and Eisenhardt, K., "Patching: Restitching Business Portfolios in Dynamic Markets", *McKinsey Quarterly*, June 2000.
11 *Growth in a Time of Uncertainty*, McKinsey, 2011.
12 Hamel, G. with Breen, B., *The Future of Management*, Harvard Business School Press, 2007.
13 Fryer, B. and Stewart, S., "Cisco Sees the Future", *Harvard Business Review*, November 2008.
14 Hastings, R. and Wells, D., "Letter to Shareholders", *Netflix Third Quarter Earnings*, Netflix, October 24th 2011.

5 Resilience

1 Margolis, J. and Stoltz, P., "How to Bounce Back from Adversity", *Harvard Business Review*, January/February 2010.
2 Warner, R., "Seven Principles of Building Resilience", *People Dynamics*, 2009.
3 Davda, A., *A Pilot Study into Measuring Resilience*, Ashridge, March 2011.
4 For further information on the Personal Resilience Questionnaire, visit www.buildingresilience.co.za
5 Davda, A., op. cit.
6 Heywood, S., Spungin, J. and Turnbull, D., "Cracking the Complexity Code", *McKinsey Quarterly*, No. 2, 2007.
7 Birkinshaw, J. and Heywood, J., "Putting Organisational Complexity in its Place", *McKinsey Quarterly*, May 2010.
8 Kleinman, M., "Horta-Osório May be the Most Ruthless Bank CEO", *Financial Times*, May 7th 2011.
9 "Back to Work for Exhausted Bank Chief", *The Times*, December 15th 2011.

6 Open collaboration

1 Hamel, M., "W.L. Gore: Lessons from a Management Revolutionary, Part 2", *Wall Street Journal*, April 2nd 2010.
2 Goodman, A., "Experiments in Employee Engagement", *Financial Times*, September 13th 2011.
3 Hamel, M., "W.L. Gore: Lessons from a Management Revolutionary, Part 1", *Wall Street Journal*, March 18th 2010.
4 *Strategic Visions on the Sourcing Market: 2012*, KPMG, 2011.
5 Edwards, C., "Why Tech Bows to Best Buy", *Bloomberg BusinessWeek*, December 10th 2009.
6 Nayar, V., *Employees First, Customers Second*, Harvard Business Press, 2010.
7 "India: Outsourcers Doing Just Fine", *Financial Times*, January 26th 2012.
8 KPMG, op. cit.
9 "Leadership After the Crisis", *Financial Times*, October 26th 2009.

10 Prahalad, C. and Venkat, R., *The Future of Competition*, Harvard Business Press, 2004.
11 Ramaswamy, R. and Gouillart, F., *The Power of Co-Creation*, Simon & Schuster Free Press, 2010.

7 Predictive learning

1 Davenport, T. and Harris, J., *Competing on Analytics: the New Science of Winning*, Accenture Institute for High Performance Business, 2006.
2 Davenport, T. and Harris, J., "Analytics and the bottom line: how organisations build success", *Harvard Business Review*, September 23rd 2010.
3 Davenport, T., Harris, J. and Morison, R., *Analytics at Work: Smarter Decisions, Better Results*, Harvard Business School Press, 2010.
4 LaValle, S. *et al.*, "Big data, analytics and the path from insights to value", *MIT Sloan Management Review*, December 21st 2010.
5 Outlined in IFTF's ten year forecast programme. For more information on the Ten-Year Forecast Programme, please contact Sean Ness at sness@iftf. org or (1) 650-233-9517.
6 Birchall, J., "B&Q Strengthens Customer Input into Business", *Financial Times*, January 11th 2011.
7 Argyris, C. and Schön, D., *Organizational learning: A theory of action perspective*, Addison Wesley, 1978.
8 Argyris, C., *Reasoning, learning, and action: Individual and organizational*, Jossey-Bass, 1982.
9 Mintzberg, H., "Rebuilding Companies as Communities", *Harvard Business Review*, July 2009.
10 Fryer, B. and Stewart, A., "Cisco Sees the Future: an Interview with John Chambers", *Harvard Business Review*, November 2008.
11 *100 Years of Foresight: The importance of long-term thinking at IBM*, IBM Centre for Applied Insights, June 2011.
12 Ibid.

8 Conclusion

1 Syrett, M., *Successful Strategy Execution: how to keep your business goals on target*, Economist Books, hardback 2007, paperback 2011.
2 Handy, C., "The Language of Leadership", *Frontiers of Leadership*, Blackwell, 1992.
3 Courtney, H., Kirkland, J. and Viguerie, P., "Strategy Under Uncertainty", *Harvard Business Review*, November–December 1997.
4 Cua, K.O., McKane, K.E. and Schroeder, R.G., "Relationship Between Implementation of TQM, JIT and TPM and Manufacturing Performance", *Journal of Operations Management*, Vol. 19, No. 6, November 2001.

Index

DATE DUE
